POST TRAUMATIC SPURS DISORDER

BEING A TOTTENHAM FAN IN THE PREMIER LEAGUE YEARS

HAYDEN GRIBBLE

Copyright © Hayden Gribble 2024

Cover illustration and kit illustration copyright © Anthony Moorin 2024

Photograph copyright © Hayden Gribble, Alison Gribble, Clara Parrish

All rights reserved

The moral rights of the author have been asserted

The right of Hayden Gribble to be identified as the author of this work has been asserted by him in accordance with the Copyright, Designs and Patents Act 1988.

This book is sold subject to the condition that it shall not, by way of trade or otherwise, be lent, resold, hired out or otherwise circulated without the publisher's prior written consent in any form of binding or cover other than that in which it is published and without a similar condition including this condition being imposed on the subsequent purchaser.

ISBN 978-1-7393752-4-9

Printed and bound by Lightning Source, Milton Keynes, United Kingdom

@hayden_gribble on Twitter/X

www.haydengribbleauthor.com

Dedicated to my Father, Alan Gribble, and my Grandfather, Herbert "Tom" Gribble.

Thanks for getting me into this mess. I mean that.

And to my children, William and Isabelle.

I'm so, so sorry...

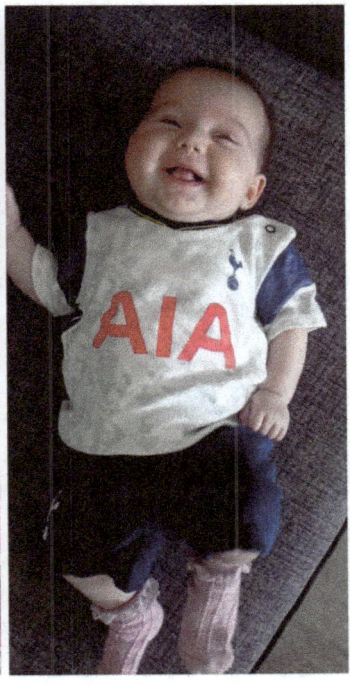

This is a book about my life as a Tottenham Hotspur supporter. All comment and analysis that isn't fact is based on the opinion of the author.
Expect swear words.

CONTENTS

My Eyes Have Barely Seen The Glory - 13
First Half - The Best Of Times - 27
1. Best Seasons - 29
2. Best Players - 85
My Best Tottenham Premier League XI - 101
3. Cult Heroes - 103
4. Best Kits - 119
5. Best Matches - 135
Half Time - 159
6. Rivalries - 161
7. The Managers - 177
Second Half - The Worst of Times - 199
8. Worst Seasons - 201
9. Worst Signings - 267
My Worst Tottenham Premier League XI - 281
10. Worst Matches - 283
11. Worst Kits - 301
12. Villains - 315
Extra Time - Books and Podcasts - 329
Acknowledgements - 337
About The Author - 341

Foreword

My Eyes Have Barely Seen The Glory

It promised so much.

Through the rose-tinted glasses of my forefathers there stood a proud, successful monument of sport in the urban streets of North London. One, that for nearly a hundred years had shone like a beacon of gold upwards towards the stars. Its luscious green turf and proud cockerel that perched adorned on the top of the west stand. The shelf. The thousands upon thousands of generations who had witnessed the glory and the glamour of the best of football and who had sung and cheered at that mighty cathedral of sport. For hours on end, my father and Grandfather would tell me stories that would drive any blossoming football fan to the verge of ecstasy. Indeed, since the 1920s it was told that my family had always frequented this incredible stadium, the pride of N17. It even had a romantic name, White Hart Lane. That wasn't where the romanticism ended either. The team that played there, in their pristine lilywhite strip also had a bloody gorgeous name too.

Tottenham Hotspur.

They were no Rovers. No United or City. Just Tottenham Hotspur. Only Queen of the South could dare to challenge it for the greatest name of a football club in Britain, perhaps the world.

For decades we Gribbles had witnessed incredible highs there at that glorious old stadium. My

Grandfather, whose name was Herbert but preferred to be called, rather confusingly, Tom, had been taken to WHL by his father in the pre-war days of the 1930s. Indeed, my Great-Grandfather could boast of being present when Spurs played Sunderland in a record capacity crowd for the old ground on the 5th March 1938, when 75,038 people witnessed an FA Cup fifth-round tie. Being local boys from Enfield, Tottenham was just a bus ride away from an afternoon of pure unadulterated escapism.

Herbert had well and truly been bitten by the bug, even wearing his Home Guard uniform to games just after the war when servicemen were allowed free entry to the ground. He also saw Arthur Rowe's push-and-run side revolutionise English football long before the likes of Arsène (spits) Wenger or Pep Guardiola.

He would sit me on his knee and tell me there had never been an inside right (whatever that was) like Len Duquemin, or an outside left (shrugs in childhood) like Sonny Walters. (Luckily when he waxed lyrical about how good Ted Ditchburn was as a player, I was on steadier ground as I heard of him and then had more cause to believe Grandad.)

When my father came along in the late 1950s, he was born into a truly golden era for the club. Bill Nicholson's side, led by Danny Blanchflower, marshalled by Dave Mackay and spearheaded by Bobby Smith, were record breakers and my dad was there for it all. He was a toddler when we won the double so sadly, didn't remember it, but before he turned ten Spurs had won one league, three FA Cups and one European Cup Winners Cup – the first

European trophy won by a British side. As he grew up, he saw two League Cup final wins and one UEFA Cup victory before it all began to go sour in the mid-seventies. Despite our relegation to the Second Division in 1977, Dad chose this time to start going to games and he loved them. Home and away my old man and his brother would watch the Spurs as they were promoted at the first attempt and evolved into cup winners yet again. He was even at Hillsborough for the 1981 FA Cup semi-final and was caught up in a crush in the Leppings Lane end – a terrifying premonition of what was to happen eight years later – but always caveated that dark story with the happier note that he, his brother and his mate hitched a ride back to Enfield on a milk float that evening.

Then he met my mother, Alison, a bank assistant and a barmaid, who just so happened to have lots of ties to Spurs. Born and brought up in nearby Harlow, my Mum went to Burnt Mill School, where Spurs legend Glenn Hoddle was in her brother's year.

Glenn once shared a rather formidable centre midfield partnership with my uncle and Mum's soon-to-be brother-in-law with team Spinney Dynamos.

Glenn himself then danced with my Nan at my Uncle Collin and Auntie Sue's engagement party! And whilst Collin went on to be signed for Southend United, captain an Australian team called Newcastle and be on the bench for Stansted FC's FA Vase win in 1984, Glenn Hoddle was never heard of again...only joking.

And that's not where the Tottenham connections end with my Mum. She was also childhood friends with Hod's first wife, Anne. Even when they were trying to get married, they took Gary Stevens and his fiancée's space at Broxbourne Church on the 16th May 1987 as that day we had the FA Cup final against Coventry and Mum's family, having originated from Leamington Spa in the Midlands all supported...you guessed it. You couldn't make it up. To this day it's the only FA Cup final we've lost and my old man was marrying into a Coventry City family on that exact day! I bet the reception was fun...

Then, just as you wouldn't think I could be any more fated to be a Spurs fan, my paternal Grandmother, Charlotte, had a brother named William Short, who as a part of the brass section, used to provide the half-time entertainment on the White Hart Lane pitch in the forties and fifties! I couldn't run, I couldn't hide. Tottenham was going to find me eventually after all those connections!

It wasn't until the summer of 1994 that I have any recollection of Spurs.

Up until then, I'd even worn my cousin's hand-me-down Liverpool shirts, not knowing what effect that was having on my poor Dad. I just thought, at that age, that wearing a red shirt with Candy on the front was fairly innocuous. But as we returned to school, and I started Year 1, five-year-old me began to partake in a celebration in the school playground called, "the Klinsmann". This involved us throwing ourselves belly first to the floor with our arms out, scuffing our knees as we went. In my primary school that year, almost all the boys had patches over their trouser knees as the Klinsmann was so popular we did it all year round.

I started to want to know more about the man who had started the craze and found to my surprise that he was a player called Jürgen Klinsmann and that he played for Tottenham Hotspur. Then I discovered that my father's entire side of the family all supported Spurs. Even my Stepgrandfather, Roy, on my mother's side, was a Spurs fan. He'd been to all the home games in the double year and was even there at Wembley on a certain day in July 1966 to watch England win the World Cup. I wanted to be a part of their club and so, despite only watching Match of the Day and England games for the next few years I started telling people that I was a Tottenham fan too.

Truthfully, I wasn't a serious fan until around our abominable 1997-98 campaign.

What a season to decide to go full-time! We stayed up thanks to my first footballing heroes David Ginola and Jürgen Klinsmann, who I was delighted came back to save us. It still took until 2000 that I understood that you could go to the games. I had never twigged that despite mates at school were going and wearing their replica shirts. I could do that too.

Sure, I collected Corinthian Prostars and their smaller counterparts called Powerpodz in the playground and also swapped Merlin Stickers to put in my book every year but the 2000-01 season was the first time that I made a proper commitment to Spurs. It was also the first time that my Dad must have noticed that this wasn't a passing phase so started investing in my new obsession. That Christmas my best present was the dark navy blue away shirt. I also got boots, which helped on those muddy secondary school pitches and I began to play every weekend for fun. I even began to get the magazine Spurs Monthly every issue, decimating it with a pair of scissors to cut out posters and photos of my new heroes in their Holsten shirts.

Then came the real clincher. I wanted to go to a game. My Dad was initially hesitant. He'd been a regular during the hooligan years and hadn't been back to White Hart Lane since the 1984 UEFA Cup final victory over Anderlecht.

A combination of cost and family got in the way of that but I'd beg him, all season round.

Then, in late April, I came home from school to find my Dad already home. There, sitting on the drinks cabinet in our living room, he alluded to me that something was sitting there I needed to see.

It was two tickets to a game against Aston Villa. I hugged him tightly and jumped around the room. I don't think I slept for the next few nights, certainly not the night before my very first game. I was so excited to be finally going to White Hart Lane. I called my Grandad and told him my happy news. We called him on the day too when we got there, something I continued to do when I went to games for many years after. I remember walking in from nearby Edmonton, seeing all those people in similar shirts to mine and holding my Dad's hand so as not to get lost. I remember buying my first scarf and my first hat at a stall near the stadium and standing on Bill Nicholson Way outside the club, Rudolphs, watching the players in their cars arrive at the ground.

Then, we entered the stadium and as I saw the lush green pitch and the cockerel sitting proudly on top of the arena I lost my breath. It was amazing. White Hart Lane looked huge. I was in heaven. The game was rubbish, sadly. We drew 0-0 and the only highlight was seeing David Ginola, though sadly now playing for the opposition.

On the way out we went to the Spurs Store and Dad bought himself the FA Cup final of 1981 against Manchester City on VHS. He explained to me that he'd been to both the final and the replay, and both in the year after too.

We watched both matches when we got home and it was far better than the crap we'd witnessed earlier!

A photo I took of Ricky Villa and Jimmy Greaves embracing at Collectormania, 2013. It has no reason to be here except that it's bloody lovely.

Dad looking on as I receive a new kit, 2003

After that, my sister Clara and I became Junior Spurs Members and by the 2001-02 season, we were semi-regulars. My Christmas presents consisted almost exclusively of Tottenham and football stuff.

The new FIFA, Match annuals, season review videos then DVDs that I'd glut on all the time.

I even used to display my matchday programmes proudly in my room too. For the next fifteen years going to Spurs was a family affair and I have been lucky enough to see us play more than fifty times.

My Dad, Mum, Clara and even little sister Rohanna would always do the pre-season friendlies in the summer as a day out. If we got a home draw in the third round of the FA Cup we'd be there too, parking up in Edmonton, or driving to Enfield and getting the train in. We'd see people we knew there and I never came away disappointed (mainly because it took until 2016 for me to see us lose in a competitive match!) Together we saw the club evolve from mid-table no-hoppers to European candidates and trophy winners. It felt so special.

Sadly, my Grandfather passed away in 2009, and he never made it to a game with me. Then in 2015, my father was diagnosed with malignant melanoma and given six months to live. Around this time his own Mother had suffered a major stroke and was barely recognisable anymore as the woman we once knew.

We were going through some dark times and then, one day, my Father said to me that the guys at work (he had been an electrician, but had spent the last couple of years being a Facilities Manager at GlaxoSmithKline in Cambridge) had spoken to the club. A signed photo and letter from Mauricio Pochettino brought a smile to all our faces. I noticed that it came from something called Spurs Wishes.

Wanting to do my own thing for Dad, I contacted them, asking if we could organise a special day out to the training ground.

My Dad had been so impressed with the new training facility in Enfield and the plans for the new stadium. So much so that one night I crept downstairs to find him on the computer looking at CGI images of what it would look like. I wanted to say thank you for all the times he took me.

My heart sank when the woman on the other end of the phone said that they couldn't do that for security purposes. But it nearly leapt out of my chest when she went on to say that she could organise him to have a box for the first home match of the season against Hull.

I was delighted. I called Dad up immediately and told him we had all been given this amazing opportunity. He was still well enough to do something like this and so for the last time as a family of five, we got in the car and he drove us to N17, through the gates and into the White Hart Lane car park.

From that moment on he was made to feel very special. He met Micky Hazard, who gave him a massive hug, John Lacy, Alan Mullery and Paul Allen. We had a meal and even a magician came to entertain us before the game started. The result was a disappointing 2-2 draw but it was Dad's experience that mattered.

The Gribble family, White Hart Lane, August 2015

Dad passed away three weeks later. I wore my 1984 Cup final shirt and his scarf to the funeral, even lay the latter on his coffin the night before. His mother passed away the day before him. In two days,y entire Spurs network had crumbled. I couldn't call any of them up to talk about the club with them anymore. They were missing so much too. The title challenges, the new stadium, Ajax!

He and my Mum had bared with me when I stood for hours queuing to meet the players when they'd do a signing in the megastore, forked out for all manner of new kits, posters, bed spreads, wall paper (my Dad decorated my room in white and navy blue with a Tottenham Hotspur freeze separating both colours. I had it from the age of 11 until 24, when I moved out!) We'd go to training days at the Lane, special shows (such as when Jimmy Greaves came to town) and friendlies. The money and effort spent by the pair of them must have been huge. So much of his passion had been handed down to me and now all that stopped. Football became a solitary experience.

Dad, with Micky Hazard and John Lacy on his final trip to White Hart Lane, 2015.

When I went to games it was now on my own. I occasionally went with a friend or two but their lives were dominated by work and family stuff now. On my latest match at the Tottenham Hotspur stadium – a 4-0 win against Huddersfield – I couldn't do it to myself anymore and gave up going altogether.

Then when my son was born in March 2021, the flame was reignited. At six months old, William became the latest in a long line of Gribbles to visit the home of the Spurs. He even got to meet Gary Mabbutt and have his nappy changed in the manager's bathroom on the tour!

Undoubtedly his little sister, Isabelle, will also come along one day and I look forward to that.

When you strip away the good and the bad, the players and managers that come and go, Tottenham Hotspur will always be about family for me. And despite my eyes not seeing the glory of my forefathers, there's still so much to enjoy and remember, many of them in this book. Across the best of times and the worst of times, this is a collection of the experiences that have made being a Spurs fan in the Premier League years so good. And bad. There are eleven in each chapter, like in a football team (geddit) and two halves of the book (again, ah!) I hope you enjoy it and that it brings back as many memories for you as it does for me. Let's all hope that the future is full of shiny silverware, eh?

COYS.

White Hart Lane: as it was for my last game there, Spurs 3-0 Bournemouth, 2016

FIRST HALF

THE BEST OF TIMES

1

BEST SEASONS

There isn't much to shout about with regards to trophies but each of these seasons showed promise and made it all the more exciting to be a fan. As time goes on you can also see the club build from mid-table to title challengers and the evolution was so fun to watch in places that it's the memories they leave behind and the players who made them so exciting, that help make a season so special...

1994/95 – Walking in a Klinsmann Wonderland...

For those who were there, the 1990s was a decade many Spurs fans would like to forget. Bookmarked by success at both ends of it, in the form of the FA Cup in 1991 and the League Cup in 1999, the rest was mostly a steaming pile of dollops. Just take a look at my picks for worst seasons and you'll understand why if you're too young to remember it all. Take it from me, though, the summer of 1994 was a brilliant one to become a Tottenham fan. However, at the time, I had no idea about the kind of trouble the club was in...

Having almost been relegated the previous campaign, the club was handed a hefty punishment for financial irregularities which occurred under the previous chairman Irving Scholar. Docked 12 points, fined

£600,000 and banned from the FA Cup for the season, it was the heaviest punishment a club in England had ever faced. Rightly so, chairman Alan Sugar appealed, citing the fact that the new regime hadn't been involved in what the club was being punished for. This led to a six-point deduction, an increase in the fine to £1.5m and we were still banned from the FA Cup!

Knowing we were pretty much doomed and facing so much adversity, Sugar needed to do something to put the smile back on Tottenham faces. He needed a name, a striker who could cushion that six-point deduction and see us safely in the Premier League the season after. And on his yacht in the South of France, he did a deal which would go down as one of the best, and most exciting, we Spurs fans have ever seen.

Do you remember where you were when we signed Jürgen Klinsmann? The World Cup winner had just come off the back of USA 94 where he had performed superbly. The German also arrived with a reputation for diving, something he joked about with the English press and they warmed to his charm immediately. At £2m his arrival was a steal and he was followed to the Lane by two stars of the Romania squad in the form of Ilie Dumitrescu from Steua Bucharest and Gica Popescu from PSV Eindhoven. The new look Spurs side didn't just look like it would avoid relegation. Manager Ossie Ardiles and his "famous five" attack of Klinsmann, Dumitrescu, Teddy Sheringham, Darren Anderton and Nick Barmby were looking to make a title challenge.

The all-out attack gameplan was exciting to watch and saw us beat Sheffield Wednesday on the opening day 4-3, with Jürgen scoring a memorable goal and performing THAT iconic celebration. Three days later, he repeated the trick with a double in a 2-1 win over Everton. After four games we were third but all the worries about the FA punishment were still hovering over White Hart Lane. Then Ossie's tactics were quickly found out and defeats to Manchester United, Southampton, Nottingham Forest, Leicester and Manchester City, not to mention a 3-0 hammering to Notts County in the League Cup, cost the Argentine his job.

Ardiles' replacement was Gerry Francis. A man with a tighter defensive plan and a mullet for all seasons. At the time his appointment seemed a good one. Having guided QPR to sixth in the Premier League's inaugural season and been linked with the England job earlier in the year, Francis sought solidity at the back and consistency.

He got it. After joining in November, we only lost another 4 games in the league from then until the end of the season. And that wasn't all. Sugar and his legal team challenged the sanctions against the club in court and the points deduction was cancelled and the ban in the FA Cup was overturned. Finally, with the ghosts of the recent past behind us, we could kick on.

In Klinsmann, we had a truly world-class talent in our squad. He formed a lethal partnership with Teddy Sheringham and a bond with the White Hart Lane faithful that remains strong to this day. Their link-up play was mouthwatering and their performances looked to be spearheading us into Europe and onto a cup final.

My biggest memories of this season come from that incredible FA Cup campaign; one we were almost so cruelly denied. I can remember our players in the yellow and bird poo kits taking on Sunderland on tele, followed by the incredible 6-2 fourth-round replay at Southampton, in which Ronnie Rosenthal became a cult hero with his hat-trick but it was the quarter-final win away at Anfield that takes me back. Sitting cross-legged on the floor looking up at the Grandstand videprinter, telling my Dad that Klinsmann had just scored a late winner against Liverpool, him punching the air and then John Motson's voice describing the game. I remember seeing our players celebrating, the fans partying, Jürgen looking emotional and the Kop applauding Spurs off the pitch! It felt huge and many back then thought that we were destined to win that brilliant trophy in a "people's final" with Manchester United.

Unsurprisingly, I don't remember the semi-final thrashing at the hands of Everton. All talk of football seemed to fizzle out of our home around then. We were dumped out unceremoniously by the Toffees, who went on to win the bloody thing, and suddenly it all began to unravel.

Klinsmann, who scored 29 goals for us that season, was named Football Writers Player of the Year and announced that at the end of the campaign, he was off back to Germany to play for Bayern Munich. Alan Sugar was so hurt that he famously said that he wouldn't even wash his car with a Klinsmann shirt.

Despite our league form being really good we finished seventh, only good enough for an Intertoto Cup place, and with Jürgen off, the dream began to die. Suddenly Popescu was out the door too to Barcelona, then even Nicky Barmby buggered off up north claiming that he was homesick. It all ended in tears but for a long time, the season was such a positive one. What a pity we didn't have one as good as this again for quite some time!

2005/06 – Martin Jol's blue and white army

Fast forwarding nearly ten years shows you just how crap it was to be a Tottenham supporter at that time. But by the mid-noughties, Dutchman Martin Jol had instilled a young and hungry squad brimming with talent and for the first time since 1985, they qualified for European football through their league placing. Of course, the season before we were robbed of the two points we needed for Europe when Pedro Mendes' incredible halfway-line effort was fumbled into the back of the net by Manchester United's Roy Carroll and wasn't given, in an astonishing moment of bad luck (then again, it was Mark Clattenburg who was ref that game, so who knows...) It could have been so much more and for so long that season, we were all dreaming of a prize much bigger than the UEFA Cup...

It all started with a glut of summer signings. Having changed our football style to be more in line with the attacking flair of teams of yesteryear, Jol's squad was boosted by the arrival of teenagers Aaron Lennon from

Leeds, Tom Huddlestone from Derby, Teemu Tainio from Auxerre, defenders Paul Stalteri and Lee Young-Pyo and exciting box-to-box midfielder Jermaine Jenas from Newcastle. Yet it was the arrival of Edgar Davids on a free from Inter Milan that got me excited. The iconic Dutchman was a world-class midfielder and was such an important signing to show our ambition and determination to do big things on the pitch.

We made a strong start to the season, scoring five and conceding none in our first three games, although the third was a goalless draw away to Blackburn. The familiar sting of defeat at the hands of Chelsea, who by now were Premier League champions, knocked us off form a bit and we didn't win another game until the end of September when Jermain Defoe sunk Fulham in a 1-0 win at White Hart Lane. That run included an embarrassing League Cup second-round defeat to Grimsby Town which I genuinely have no memory of. Considering I was still an obsessive with not much else going on in my life at the time, it must have been bad for all but the result to be sponged from memory.

But back in the league, we were showing some consistency. In fact, up until the end of the year, we had only lost three games. It was unthinkable territory for us back then. Sure, we had a great young side but to be this far up the league with half the season played it was incredible, but there was a genuine feeling of something special happening. In Robinson, Dawson, King, Carrick, Jenas, Lennon and Defoe we had a core of young exciting English players blended with the international experience of Lee, Davids, Stalteri and

Mido, not to mention Robbie Keane, who had cut a frustrating figure around the start of the year. It was rumoured that he had a punch-up with Davids on the training pitch and hadn't been in Jol's plans much throughout 2004 as Defoe and Mido were his preferred striking options.

However, once he got back in the side, Keano seized his chance and ended up scoring 16 league goals – his highest return for us to this point – and becoming vice-captain in Ledley King's absence. The young side seemed to know no fear, giving a great account for themselves in 1-1 draws away to Manchester United and at home against the Scum, where Stalteri thought he was fouled by Dennis Bergkamp in the build-up to their equaliser and stopped playing instead of playing to the whistle. That's something we knew to do in the return fixture but more on that later.

It was during this season that I was in my first and only year of sixth form. My interests in music and cricket had meant that my bedroom – which was once adorned by Spurs players, now saw the likes of Ledley King rubbing shoulders with the likes of Freddie Flintoff and Thom Yorke! But because I was living off EMA money at the time (the £10 you got from the government every week for attending further education) and now my sisters were growing up, money was tight so we didn't go at all to White Hart Lane this campaign and so I solely relied on friends who had Sky Sports and trying to get in the pub to watch it. Sadly, although my first job that summer had been in the pub kitchen it was quite on and off. I was never anywhere near the tele and at that point, the pub didn't have Sky. I listened to the North London Derby whilst peeling spuds! Plus, the second pub in our village knew I was 16 so I couldn't go in without my Dad.

So my two most memorable viewing moments occurred away from White Hart Lane. I was ecstatic that our place within the top four had lasted from Christmas until April and with less than ten games to go, it looked like we were going to do it. Our nearest rivals, Blackburn, had fallen at White Hart Lane to a brilliant solo Keane goal and the Scum, who were scarily looking good in the Champions League, looked like dollop in the league and were miles behind us it felt. For game 29 that year, I sat in my Chelsea friend's front room to see us give a really good account of ourselves against his lot. They were marching to a second consecutive league title but with the game a 1-1 going into added time, it looked like we'd shown our mettle. Yet, as was so common this season, we conceded in stoppage time to a long-range William Gallas goal and I proceeded to try and smother my friend with a pillow to stop him goading me.

Then there was the final visit to the Lighbury. The Gooners had snuck back on us and were about to book their place in the Champions League final. Once again, my old man had to work a weekend shift but in his new job, there was a bar with the football on. I begged him to let me go and watch it and since it was a research facility in Cambridge, and it was a Saturday, the place was dead. I got to watch the NLD in a deserted bar, with only my dad poking his head around the door between jobs to see what the score was!

A collision between two Goons in the build-up to Robbie Keane's opener led to a touchline spat between Arsey Winger and Martin Jol. There was no reason for us to put the ball out of play, the referee hadn't blown his whistle, and so from my viewpoint, there was nothing to moan about.

As the seconds ticked down it looked like we were going to ruin our rival's final-ever derby game at their old ground until Henry equalised late on but we were superb that day.

I remember nearly breaking a chair when Carrick went on a Ricky Villa-style run and then hit the side netting.

After the 1-0 win against Bolton on the penultimate day it was confirmed that no matter what, Spurs were back in Europe again. Okay, so we only played 40 games all season, the bare minimum (that 3-2 defeat to Leicester in the FA Cup was toe-curling) but I was so proud of the players and of course, Martin Jol, who everyone I knew seemed to love.

Even after the horrendous goings on during the final day (see Worst Moments) for the first time in my life I felt truly proud to be a Spurs fan.

It gave everyone a shot in the arm and to make up for no games that season we went on a tour that summer of White Hart Lane.

I remember standing in the directors' box looking up at the golden cockerel dreaming of European nights. A few months later, they would be a reality...

Rohanna, myself and Mum in the dressing room, the Tottenham tour, 2006

"One day, all of this will be mine…" in front of the hallowed turf, 2006

2006/07 – We're all going on a European tour!

What a summer. For Spurs we signed Dimitar Berbatov from Bayer Leverkusen, Didier Zokora from Saint-Etienne, Benoit Assou-Ekotto from Lens, Steed

Malbranque from Fulham and Pascal Chimbonda, who had impressed so much at right-back for Wigan that he had made the PFA Team of the Year. Sadly, we lost one of our shining lights from the season before in Michael Carrick who was convinced to go north to Manchester United in an £18m deal, a record outgoing. I was gutted. There I had been checking the papers at my local shop for news and then I saw it. Dismayed, but Carrick wasn't the only one who was making a move.

After months of my Mum telling me to, I had decided that I'd get out into the daunting world of college and train to be a plumber rather than continue in sixth form. Sure, I loved writing but my thinking was that if I never made it as a journalist (the places in the college were full for that course) at least I could make a living out of fixing boilers and replacing taps. The guys on the course were mostly a year younger than me, fresh out of school, but a nice bunch of working-class lads who all spoke my language. In between unsuccessfully trying to chat up the girls in the hairdressing classes near us, we'd talk about the footie, music and booze. A 17-year-old's dream! And since there were no Gooners or Chelsea fans in the class, just West Ham, Millwall and Man Utd, no one could give me any stick over the sick bug at the end of the previous season, try as the Hammer might!

Which was good, because we were awful domestically at the start of that season. In fact, by the start of October, we'd only won one game in the league; a 2-0 win over newly promoted Sheffield United. It was also the only game we had scored in!

But I didn't mind because my Thursday nights had just got exciting as we were back in Europe. Whether it was Channel 5 or ITV2, there was no disappointment that we were only in Europe's secondary competition, but unbridled joy, because we hadn't been there in years and, we had pedigree in the competition. Two 1-0 wins over Slavia Prague over two legs, followed by group victories against Besiktas, Bruge, Bucharest and Bayer Leverkusen saw us through to the knockout round with a 100% record! And what's more, Berbatov had come alive in Europe and looked like the best striker we'd had on our books since Klinsmann.

By Christmas, he already had ten goals to his name. That was almost unheard of in the eleven years that had passed since Sheringham and Klinsmann had done the business upfront. For Spurs to have strikers who could get 20 goals a season was an absolute dream and Berba was proving to be that man. Jermain Defoe was out to prove a point too, as he capitalised on an injury to Robbie Keane that saw him show England what they had been missing after Sven Goran Eriksen had made the ridiculous decision to take a teenage Theo Walcott, who hadn't kicked a ball in the Premier League, instead of him for the 2006 World Cup.

Slowly but surely, we began to rebuild our domestic form with the highlight being our fantastic 2-1 win over Josè Mourinho's Chelsea on Bonfire Night. For the first time in 16 years, we'd done them in the league, putting to rest a stupid hoodoo that lot seemed to have over us. As I watched the game at my Chelsea friend's house, surrounded by HIS blue mates, I kept schtum throughout. The moment Ledley raced back to thwart Robben I gasped. Makelele's wonder strike? I flopped in my chair. Dawson's equaliser picked me back up again and then when young Aaron Lennon cut inside and put us 2-1 up, I gripped the chair so hard I nearly turned it to splinters. When John Terry was sent off I did allow myself to celebrate a little but this was Spurs and even back then, I knew it wasn't over until the whistle blew. When it did, I was insufferable with my celebrations, so much so that the host chased me out of the house with a bat!

In the cups, we went deep in every competition. Quarter-finals of the FA Cup (dumped out by Chelsea after a replay in which Anthony Gardner failed to clear a ball in the last minute owing to having just broken his leg), the Scum in the League Cup in the Semi-finals (after Ricardo Rocha showed us exactly why we shouldn't have bought him as two costly errors saw that lot go through) and, sadly, downed by Sevilla in the UEFA Cup in the quarter-finals. Our fans had suffered a torrid time in Spain having been beaten by the police and back in the home leg our confidence was soon shattered when Malbranque buried it in his own net and former player Freddie Kanoute doubled their advantage. We fought back to draw the home tie but the European dream was over.

That's when things in the league started to perk up. After a rocky January, we were in the bottom half and with 11 games to go, Sheffield United had just beaten us 3-1. Man Utd, who at one point had defender John O'Shea in goal, had just thrashed us 4-0 too. There were also whispers that chairman Daniel Levy was getting fed up and had started to scout for a new manager. In the face of all this adversity, we turned on the style, losing just one of our remaining 11 games in the league (a narrow 1-0 defeat to, yes, Chelsea again), and winning eight, including that fantastic comeback at Upton Park.

West Ham looked good to go down but had shocked us with an early two-goal cushion but we had clawed it back through Defoe and Tainio before former Spur Bobby Zamora smashed a header past Paul Robinson with five minutes to go. We struck back again with Berbatov squeezing a brilliant free-kick into the top corner with a minute on the clock. In the final minute, Defoe broke free and saw his low shot parried by Rob Green straight to the feet of Paul Stalteri who couldn't miss. The away end exploded. I nearly punched the light out above me in our living room from celebrating and Spurs, who had a reputation for conceding late, had only gone and snatched it whilst condemning the Hammers to relegation, it seemed.

On the final day, I watched Soccer Saturday on the tele in my room, waiting for our scoreline at home to Manchester City to come in. We finished the game 2-1 victors, meaning that we had finished 5th for the second consecutive year. With another run in Europe to look forward to and a squad which had scored 101 goals in the season (even goalie Paul Robinson got in on the act against Watford, memorably beating Ben Foster from his own box!) the next thing to tick off for my Dad and I was a trophy. Turns out, we didn't have long to wait...

2009/10 - 'Arry steers us to fourth and the Champions League awaits…

Picking up a strange kind of bird at the football, 2009

After a couple of years of there being some worrying inconsistency at the club, 2009/10 has to be, in my mind, the most fun I've ever had as a Spurs fan. For the first time in years, I was able to go to games again, having purchased my membership. I also decided that plumbing wasn't for me and instead spent two years working in a camping shop in Saffron Walden. I'd also enrolled in journalism college in Harlow, meaning I got to mix with lots of fellow Spurs fans. Add to that

I'd attended Reading Festival that summer and already had my ticket for the fourth game of the season at home to Birmingham, I looked at all the predictors in the papers and scoffed. They all said that owing to Tottenham's up-and-down season last time out, where we eventually finished 8th, we wouldn't get higher than 6th this time out.

But after four games we had a 100% record. It was the best in my lifetime, taking in a 2-1 victory over Liverpool (now being 20 years old, I could watch and drink in the pub and this was a standout game in my local because of the number of Spurs fans there!), a 5-1 mauling of Hull away (I missed that for a cinema trip instead, idiot), a 2-1 late win over West Ham then I was there to see us win 2-1 over the Brummies. Well, I say that, most of it. We outclassed them that day but just couldn't seem to score. Sitting just to the right of the goal in row 1 in the Paxton, I watched chance after chance pass us by. New signing Peter Crouch finally put us in front, only for Craig Gardner to equalise late and I stormed off. More fool me. As soon as I'd started walking down the High Road, a huge roar went up from the crowd still inside White Hart Lane. Myself and my fellow deserters stopped like we were playing musical statues, disbelieving, until a cabbie drove past us honking his horn yelling, "Lennon's scored!" To further my education in staying until the final whistle, on that night's Match of the Day the camera kept showing me, to my parents' delight! Then to punish me further, a camera angle of Lennon's goal froze framed and showed my stark, empty seat. Since that day I've never left before the end as in football, you just never know!

For the rest of it, we were pretty consistent. We didn't fall lower than sixth all season. There were the customary losses to the big boys as Manchester United, Chelsea and the Scum all won comfortably against us early on and the off slip-up against Stoke and Wolves, but there was confidence amongst Harry Redknapp's men, a cavalier, swashbuckling type of football that was seeing goals galore. Jermain Defoe scored five in the incredible 9-1 hammering of Wigan, Robbie Keane bagged four in a 5-0 mauling of Burnley and Peter Crouch bagged a hat-trick in the League Cup versus Preston. It was in the next round I made another pilgrimage to the Lane with my mate Dan, who told me after I'd got the train there from college, that there were no trains after the game for some reason. Throughout the game, I panicked and also had no bars of reception on my mobile. Then I spotted my neighbours in a part of the Park Lane end! I shouted over to ask if I could get a lift and after our 2-0 victory over Everton I met them outside the stand. Unfortunately, my neighbour Paul had a full quota for the car but said that if I didn't mind I could jump in the boot. So, there I was, with my head up on the wheel arch, phone torch in my mouth to read the programme as I bumped my way down the M11 back to Essex thinking what a laugh it all was!

I even took my girlfriend to the Leeds United FA Cup tie in January. Sadly, she was a little clueless about the game, even turning to me and making me laugh when Crouch scored for us saying, "Is that good?" when the 36,000 people surrounding her were jumping for joy. She was a funny one! As we trudged back from the 2-2 draw we got caught up in train cancellations again and didn't get home until 1am that night. But it was all a part of the fun that we were watching and after Christmas, I became convinced that without the following four players coming in and stepping up when first-teamers we're out injured, we wouldn't have tasted the success that we did at the end. They were Gareth Bale, David Bentley, Nico Kranjcar and Roman Pavlyuchenko. None of them was in 'Arry's plans when the likes of Assou-Ekotto, Lennon, Modrić and Defoe were playing but they all came in, got crucial goals and by the end of the season we realised just how much strength in depth we had.

It was all coming down to a make-or-break April. To qualify for the Champions League for the first time, we had to get results against the Gooners, Chelsea, Man Utd, Bolton (who were a bit of a bogey team for us) then go to nearest rivals Manchester City and get something there. That task was made all the more unlikely after we lost the FA Cup semi-final to Portsmouth. I was so pissed off I wanted to avoid the North London Derby just a few days later, dreading what the result would be. So I hid at my girlfriend's house. Then I had a text from my Mum saying that Danny Rose had scored. Who? Why was he playing? What was the goal like? Then after a brief break in conversation, she texted me again to tell me that Bale had put us two up! We hurriedly made for the nearest pub to watch the rest of the game. I had to endure that back-to-the-wall performance in the final half hour of the game, as we clung onto our lead. Gomes was unplayable that night in undoubtedly his best performance in a Spurs shirt and despite a late Van Persie goal, we held on.

Our first league victory over that lot since 1999.

And Rose's goal had been an absolute belter! I promised myself that I'd pay closer attention to the Chelsea game that Saturday.

Again, we won 2-1! It was unbelievable. Earlier on in the day in the Manchester derby, Paul Scholes had scored a last-minute winner over their rivals Man City, so if we beat our enemies then there would be some breathing room.

Bale was unstoppable again and John Terry was sent off against us again so all-in-all, phone conversations in the debrief with my Spurs friends and family members were chipper.

In the end, we did it. It was an evening to remember. Crouch's goal, 'Arry's soaking in the post-match interview seemingly putting a nail in Bentley's career with us and then we had a record SIX players called up for England at the World Cup that summer.

For the first time in yonks, there were no high-profile departures, only the promise of a great summer and an exciting season mixing it with the elite of European football the following term.

The state of just a part of my bedroom wall with signatures from players, 2010

2010/11 – The Glory Glory Nights return

After the adventures of the previous campaign, in my personal life, it was a bit of a bump back to Earth. In the late summer, my father was diagnosed with skin cancer. Having just turned 50, and I was 21, it felt all too early to be worrying about my parents health and yet there I was, mulling over all kinds of things at a time when I should have been kicking on, much like Spurs had. My relationship ended too, as did my journalism course and by Christmas I was a worker for hire at Addenbrookes Hospital, being a security guard in the Special Care Baby Unit while trying to get sports writer jobs! But with all the worry and stress that had appeared in my personal life, having Spurs back was a blessed relief.

Pity then that domestically we started really meh. Out in the League Cup falling at the first hurdle to the Scum in a 4-1 home defeat and suffering patchy form, only Gareth Bale's stellar performances were bringing me sunshine. We even nearly cocked up our Champions League campaign with a 3-2 defeat away to Young Boys in Switzerland on the infamous plastic pitch. Luckily, Crouchy scored a hat-trick past them in the home leg and we began to lick our lips after being drawn in Group A along with reigning champions Inter Milan, FC Twente from Holland and Werder Bremen from Germany.

The summer signings had been a little lacklustre with young Sandro moving to N17 and William Gallas controversially joining on a free from the Scum. On deadline day, we shocked the world by bringing the mercurial talents of Rafael Van der Vaart through the door. The Dutch International was a magician and immediately formed a bond with the fans and a partnership with Crouch up front, with Defoe out for most of the early season and Robbie Keane having fallen behind Roman Pavlyuchenko in the pecking order.

Pub trips abound this season and my old man managed to make most of them with me as I wanted to not go to the games without him until he felt he could go again. Together, surrounded by Spurs fans, we watched our adventures in the Champions League. The 2-2 draw away to Werder Bremen was exhilarating, if not a little disappointing after the Germans had clawed back a share of the points. Then the 4-1 win over FC Twente, with Super Pav and VdV instrumental in victory nicely setting up a trip to the San Siro to play the mighty Inter. As this one was ITV, we watched as a family at home and felt like turning over when we went 4-0 and ten men down by half-time. But Gareth Bale's masterclass in the second half not only restored pride but announced him as a true talent on the greatest domestic platform there is. We celebrated every goal like it was a winner and then, going into the return fixture, there was no fear. My Dad and I were celebrating down the local for the 3-1 win on a night that showed me exactly what the term Glory, Glory Night had been invented for.

The league form was getting better too, as we completed our first win over the Gooners at the Emirates 3-2, after going 2-0 down in the first half. Then Aaron Lennon scored a late winner against Liverpool at home to show that the Inter performances were no fluke. Harry Redknapp's team was coming of age and were pushing all connotations of us having a soft underbelly (people would later call it being "S****y" but thankfully that phrase hadn't been coined yet) firmly back in the face of our doubters.

The going was still good in the Champions League as we beat AC Milan 1-0 at the San Siro this time in a mature performance with many of our first-teamers unavailable. Modrić was only fit enough to be on the bench but his toe poke to Aaron Lennon, who steamed down the right and gave the usually unflappable Alessandro Nesta a panic attack before squaring it to Crouch who fluffed his shot but it still nestled in the bottom corner of the net. We clung on and the handbags from Genaro Gattuso (and the head butt on

Joe Jordan at the end) meant we had won the psychological battle as well as the physical one. Sadly, Crouchy lost his head early in the quarter-final away to Real Madrid and saw red, as we lost 4-0. Eventually that tie proved one step too far but the boys had done us proud in their debut season at the head table of European football. Now, we just had to get there again.

This was proving tricky. Back at home Man City's oil money was starting to be pumped through the club, better equipping them for the run-in. In the repeat fixture of the game at the Etihad the previous year, we found ourselves losing 1-0 this time and with three games to go, being condemned to 5th in the table, unable to break into the top 4. Sadly, we drew too many games this season. Despite losing only 8 games compared to the 10 in the previous year, we drew 14 fixtures and that's what cost us. In the end, City had pushed on, eventually finishing 3rd and winning the FA Cup. We made do with our place back in the UEFA Cup, now rebranded as the Europa League and consolidated it by going to Anfield and beating Liverpool 2-0 then relegating Birmingham City (who had embarrassed the Gooners by beating them late on in the League Cup final) to the Championship.

As the Gribble family wolfed down their Sunday lunch watching that game with my Father, now in remission, I hoped I'd get back to the Lane more next year as a battle to keep our best players began and our arch-rivals reared their ugly head...

2011/12 – Fourth again but England want 'Arry, while Levy wants Nelson and Saha...

You've got a Freund in me...JJ and Steffen with me, 2012

Following my season-long sabbatical from White Hart Lane I more than made up for my absence in this season. In total, I attended twelve league games, two cup matches and three European ties. The ticket exchange proved to be a cheap and cheerful way of getting me to the Lane and with my dad still wanting to stay away for a bit I was now going solo. But what a campaign 2011-12 was to watch. Possibly the most dramatic for nearly twenty years, we saw Chelsea try to prize Luka Modrić away for an eye-watering £40m only for Daniel Levy to turn down their advances. Then our opening fixture against Everton was postponed due to the riots in Tottenham (I had a ticket for that game AND the cancelled England international at Wembley against Holland). We started by getting thrashed by both Manchester clubs with an aggregate score of 9-1, with the only consolation that United destroyed the Scum 8-2 in an afternoon that saw North London truly sunk by the Mancs.

In pre-season, we had been busy with Forty-year-old keeper Brad Friedel joining for a free along with Scott Parker from West Ham for £5.5m. The Football Writers Player of the Year as the Hammers had gone down, Parker was a shrewd signing as Wilson Palacios was moved on to Stoke along with Peter Crouch. His place up front was filled by another controversial signing from 'Arry. Emmanuel Adebayor, who a season earlier had well and truly stuck it to his old fans when he scored for Manchester City against the Scum, joined on a season-long loan and caused a bit of a stir as he became the second former Gooner in our line-up alongside William Gallas.

But his signing proved a masterstroke as we went on an unbeaten run of 14 league games, playing some fantastic, free-flowing football along the way. We only lost three times in our opening 21 league matches in a special start to the season that had some of us dreaming of a title tilt. Why not when you have the likes of Bale, Modrić and Van der Vaart, world-class players doing the business? We even had the luxury of playing the reserves in the Europa League as Redknapp prioritised our domestic chances but gave invaluable first-team experience to our stars of tomorrow. The likes of Harry Kane, Danny Rose, Andros Townsend, Tom Carroll and Jake Livermore all played a part in the group stage which we sadly failed to escape and progress from.

In January we succumbed to Man City in a sliding doors game. Having gone 2-0 down we pulled it back through Bale and Defoe then troubled Italian striker Mario Balotelli stamped on Scott Parker's head but the incident was missed by the referee so he stayed on the pitch. In the dying moments, Bale put a delicious ball across the six-yard box for Defoe to tap in, but the striker's small frame could do nothing but let it brush his studs to go wide in a moment eerily reminiscent of Gazza for England against Germany in Euro 96. Then up the other end, Ledley, who by this point was held together by glue and some sticky back plastic, upended Balotelli in the box and the striker scored from the spot to send us 3-2 down when really, we deserved to win.

What we needed was some added quality in our squad. Redknapp wanted Eden Hazard and Gary Cahill, both great players who hadn't been discovered by the big boys yet. Levy delivered him Ryan Nelson and Luis Saha…two experienced journeymen who were past their best. What a let down that transfer window was…

But we weren't down in the dumps for long. Later that month our manager was cleared of tax evasion but in a cruel moment of timing, England boss Fabio Capello quit after a row over John Terry not being allowed to captain the side after his alleged racist incident with Anton Ferdinand earlier in the season. Now 'Arry was a wanted man for a completely different reason and in our home game against

Newcastle, all the songs from the fans were about wanting Redknapp – the architect of all our fun over the last few years – to stay. That day I packed up my Ford Fiesta, put 'The Best of The Police' in my CD player and pooted up the M11 to Harlow train station. Just as I always did for games on my own, I'd park up, get the train to Northumberland Park and walk down the stadium and all the way it felt like we as fans had a job to do to convince Harry to stay.

We ended up blowing Newcastle out of the stadium that day in a 5-0 hammering. Going home I thought that Police CD was good luck. For the next four years, I played it, both journeys there and back, and we didn't lose once (until Monaco did us at Wembley in 2016). If I'd told the club, maybe they'd have given me a season ticket and Sting an executive box!

Despite that result, with the manager and certain players futures spiralling around the press, our form tanked. A defeat to the Scum, who had been struggling up until that point, started a run of games that saw us win 4 of our last 12 matches. Luckily, because our form had been so good up until then it guaranteed us fourth place, which every season was enough to see us safely back in the Champions League. But all was not well. Ledley, like Boxer in Animal Farm, was finished, Modrić didn't want to be there (I watched him refuse to take set pieces and shirk runs in our 3-1 against Swansea, at one point overhearing Van der Vaart telling him to, "pull yourself together you moody f****r", and 'Arry looked nailed on for the England job. Then the FA, in their infinite wisdom, played the safe card again and appointed Roy

Hodgson, thus derailing our season for no good reason.

Then there was the tragic Fabrice Muamba moment. The Bolton midfielder had a cardiac arrest during our FA Cup quarter-final at the Lane and for a long time was clinically dead on the White Hart Lane turf. It was a shocking incident, one I had missed as I didn't get a ticket in time, but one I was watching unfold on TV. The fans were fantastic, willing the medics to push to resuscitate him. Then referee Howard Webb abandoned the match, rightly so, and we all prayed for Muamba to make it. Thankfully, he did and our boys joined the footballing world in wishing him good health in our next game over Stoke. It was in that game that tensions in the crowd boiled over and I had to step in to stop a fight in the normally quiet Paxton Road end. It was picked up by security and later that week, I had a surprise call from the club asking me for my view on what had happened! Maybe they had my number because I was a fan, I don't know, but in the end, it was just handbags at dawn and nothing happened. My cheeky request for a free ticket to the next game as a reward for being a good Samaritan fell on deaf ears, sadly!

On the final day, I watched from my usual seat, behind the goal of the Paxton Road end, a couple of rows up as we needed to match the Gooner's result to finish 4th. We'd been here before but this time, we won 2-0, comfortably securing the Champions League for next season but sadly letting that lot finish a point above us. That was the day of the amazing Man City/QPR game and as Aguero scored, cheers went up in the ground and I watched people celebrating in the boxes. This was a true vindication of how much the Red Devils were hated at the time, that's for sure!

Sadly, the fate of our season rested in the hands of Chelsea. We all know what happened next (see Worst Moments) and within a matter of weeks, the Harry Redknapp years came to a crushing end as he was dismissed by Daniel Levy. What a few years it had been though. The style of football, the achievements on the pitch. It had all been such an incredible ride and I'd seen so much of it as the club had evolved.

Now, though, it was all about the top 4 every season, for reasons of Spurs competing with their rivals and keeping our best players.

The fun element had slowly ebbed away when it came to league games and my excitement was now feeling tempered by a fear of nerves that every game needed to be a must-win.

The 'Rule the Roost' podcast said the same thing on one of their shows talking about this time and it's so true.

To everyone who was there, this era felt like the time when the club became a contender and so playtime was over.

It conjures so much. The clap of the seats as Lennon got to the byline, the smell of the burger vans. McNamara's Band getting me going every time. I loved it all.

We had to put our toys away and grow up to be taken seriously. Subsequently, the next few years were tough as we tried to push forward and it would take a new manager and new team to take us on another exhilarating adventure...

Me, brother-in-law Jordan and sister Clara at a game, 2013

2015/16 – He's magic, you know...

Football is the escape of the working man. At least it was in the olden days. You worked all week, finished just in time for the 3pm kick-off and it would take all your cares away. For ninety minutes you would be invested in the game and all your troubles could melt into the ether. In this season, watching Spurs was both a tonic and a painful reminder of what we as a family had just lost.

In the space of 24 hours, both my father and my grandmother passed away. Just three weeks after our family day out to the first home game of the season, Dad was gone. The thing that kept me closest to him, the constant that we bonded over the most was football, and Spurs in particular. Now every time I watched a game it was both a relief and a pained sadness that he wasn't here anymore. When he announced to us earlier in the year about his diagnosis, to try and cut the atmosphere I said, "Well, sorry to say this, Dad, but I don't think Spurs will be winning the Premier League in the next six months." He laughed and responded in kind. "I could live another 70 years and I still wouldn't see them win it!" Oh Dad, this season, we were closer than we'd been in decades...

If anything, Tottenham's form felt a bit like a gift from the heavens. We had a very young side but it was just as exciting as anything we'd had since the Harry Redknapp days and in a season where Manchester United, the Scum and Chelsea were all having to rebuild after a change in management or playing staff, or both, we took our opportunity to snatch Champions League qualification back. This also included some positive results. Despite not winning any of our first four games (drawing three) our campaign got going after a 4-1 mauling of Manchester City at the Lane. It was also the first game in which Harry Kane, who was being labelled a one-season wonder after his 31 goals the previous year, got off the mark and I will always remember where I watched it.

I took myself off for the day to London and found myself in Whitechapel. Knowing that the game was kicking off soon, I ducked into the nearest boozer, well aware that I was in West Ham territory and not wanting to cause any trouble. As I saddled up at the bar, I noticed the claret and blue decor all around me then a decoration on the wall which had a photo of the Kray twins (for anyone who doesn't know, they were notorious gangsters in the sixties who were jailed for violent crimes). Suddenly, it twigged where I was. This was The Blind Beggar. The pub where Ronnie Kray shot George Cornell and was later sentenced to life imprisonment. With this newfound information, and the Hammers fans filling up for drinks before their game that day, I suddenly felt very vulnerable.

I had no problems in the end. It turned out to be one of the friendliest pubs I've ever been in! Even after they realised I was a Spurs fan (celebrating four goals may have given it away) there were no dramas!

It was an early highlight for a season of many. I missed some of our matches as I went on a trip to the United States for two weeks in October, a day after my dad's funeral. I'd also recently started seeing someone too, who had given me the choice to cool things off while my personal life was going through lots of turmoil. I said no, wanting to grab the things which made life good with both hands and not let them go. Four years later, I married her! It was a bit of a bonus when she told me that she was distantly related to Nick Barmby! I then proudly informed her that I had a Corinthian figure of him under the bed. What she made of that I've never asked!

Thrashing Bournemouth, West Ham and Norwich all before Christmas, this team was beginning to excite me. It was when I was at my new girlfriend, Sophie's parents' house that the penny started to drop on just where we could be going this season. When Son scored a late winner against Watford, we were 4th in the league, one which was being dominated amazingly by Leicester City. But I suddenly had this realisation that we could potentially enter a title race. As we lost to the Foxes soon after, I still thought we could push the unlikely league leaders, although the Scum had been top at Christmas but looked a little wobbly themselves.

After watching us thrash Sunderland 4-1, I invited my Mum over to watch the game at Crystal Palace where we saw the birth of generational talent Dele Alli as a quality player. His flick up, spin and volley from the edge of the box had us both up and out of our seats. Then when Nacer Chadli curled one into the net to make the game safe, we rose to third and the title challenge was well and truly on!

It wasn't hard juggling a new relationship with my football obsession. I even decided to prioritise Valentine's Day over our away fixture at the Etihad with Man City, although I did keep checking my phone and whooped when I saw that a Christian Eriksen goal had given us a priceless 2-1 win. Our brilliant form was interrupted once again by a disappointing defeat away to West Ham, but when the North London Derby rolled up next, I was away in Cardiff, again having to resort to my phone for updates due to commitments. For 12 minutes, a Harry Kane goal which defied belief sent us top. We were destined for 1st for the first time all season until the Gooners equalised late on. It was even more annoying considering they had played most of the second half with ten men. Our chance had gone but I was sure there would be more.

Then came my last game at old White Hart Lane. I went with my best mate and later best man Briggers, first for a pint in the Bill Nick, then on to say goodbye to the old stadium as the builders were just starting to move in. A 3-0 win was a great send-off for my last time there, although at the time I thought I'd be able to go again. Then started a bizarre run of fixtures where Leicester played on the Saturday and we kept being given the Sky televised game on the Sunday or Monday, meaning that whatever ground we needed to catch up, it put more pressure on us. I started to wonder if all neutrals wanted us to lose ground so that Leicester could get their fairytale. By the end of that 2-2 draw at Stamford Bridge, it was clear as day that nobody, except us, wanted Spurs to win the title.

Then came those crushing defeats to Southampton and Newcastle, the final game a 5-1 thrashing at the hands of a side who had been relegated and a result which meant the Gooners (who had been top at Christmas, remember?) pipped us to 2nd place. Queue the memes, the phrase "S***sy" being bantered around and the ridicule. But sod that, we'd only lost six games, amassed 69 points and were back in the mixer for the first time since the 1980s. There was no doubt that we'd progressed. Kane wasn't a one-season wonder, we were back in the Champions League and going into the final season at White Hart Lane, and we had a manager who was magic, you know...

2016/17 – Premier League runners-up and it's the end of the Lane

In the vast majority of seasons that came before this one, 86 points would have seen the club who had reached that incredible total with the Premier League trophy in their cabinet. How cruel is it now, to look back and see this as the peak of Mauricio Pochettino, in which we won that amount of points and went unbeaten at home all season just to finish 2nd? Our hated rivals Chelsea beat us to the top of the tree with 93 points, under Antonio Conte, playing a boring style of football that was robotic and sedate. We, however, were playing with style, attacking, offensive football and we scared every club that we came up against. We scored 86 goals and only conceded 26 with the best for and against record in the entire league. This was a side that deserved to be champions.

I barely missed a game, managing to watch on TV and also making four trips to Wembley, discovering the best curry house I have ever been to (Gurkha Valley in Wembley, you were brilliant!) and wore my shirt with pride everywhere I went. I was prouder than ever to be a Spurs fan as our side beat Man City, Man Utd, the Gooners, Chelsea and beat sides by more than three goals no less than 11 times, including finishing our season with a 6-1 hammering of Leicester and 7-1 against relegated Hull, with Harry Kane scoring seven in them to romp home the Golden Boot for the second consecutive year.

We beat the Scum in the final North London Derby at the Lane and in doing so, meant that we'd finish above them for the first time since 1995, leaving their stupid St Totteringham's Day jibes firmly in the bin. We went unbeaten for the first 12 games of the season, a feat not seen since the Bill Nicholson side won the double. It was a monumental year to be a Spurs fan and all it needed to round everything off was a trophy.

I was convinced that even if we weren't going to catch Chelsea in the league (their 14-game winning streak earlier in the season pretty much won them the title) we were going to do them when we drew them in the FA Cup. So much so that I went to the game, yet Wembley hadn't been a happy hunting ground for us since the 2008 League Cup win. We'd lost two of our Champions League games there to Monaco and Bayer Leverkusen, only beating CSKA Moskow who finished bottom of that group. But as I went up the escalators to my seat, I felt we'd do it. Then the team news came in...to say that Mauricio Pochettino's greatest failing was that he failed to take cup competitions seriously was an understatement here and sadly, I left Wembley deflated.

Nick, my friend from journalism college and me on semi-final day, Wembley, 2017

There's a cruel irony that our best side since the 1960s, certainly the best of the Premier League era, never won anything as a team. You can argue that it's got harder to win with so many clubs already having a modern-day reputation for trophies and with the financial doping that Chelsea and Man City have enjoyed. I took my hope that we'd win something into the following season and just preferred to remember how bloody brilliant this season was. I moved in with Sophie at the end of it, buying a house together and officially gave up freelance football journalism at this time too. I was ready to watch as a fan again and couldn't wait for a summer of quality signings and the excitement of a new stadium being built whilst in the meantime having Wembley as our temporary home.

Wemberley, Wemberley! Me wearing Dad's old scarf, 2017

2017/18 – Spurs are on their way to Wembley

Considered contenders for the league title for the first time, it took us a while to adapt to playing at Wembley as the club brought in four faces to boost the squad but the cracks were starting to show. Star right-back Kyle Walker had told Poch back in Spring that he wanted to leave and a £50m deal to Man City was struck. Then Danny Rose went public with his criticism of the club's transfer dealings, stating that he didn't want to be "Googling" the names that we were linked to and wanted to see us showing ambition. He was right, and perhaps the likes of Juan Foyth, Paulo Gazzaniga and Serge Aurier weren't the type of names that he wished were coming in. Spanish veteran Fernando Llorente was probably on the wrong side of 30 and it had been nearly a decade before we'd finally got him on our books after being linked back in 2010, but overall the squad now had more depth to deal with a better run on all fronts.

The style of football was the same as the year before and we wiped the floor with some of our closest rivals at the top. We thrashed Liverpool in a 4-1 win at Wembley in October which set us on our way at home plus won our first away game at Chelsea for nearly thirty years. We crushed Josè Mourinho's Manchester United 2-0, with Eriksen scoring after ten seconds. We beat the Scum 1-0 at a record turnout for a Premier League game where 83,222 people saw Harry Kane score, and Erik Lamela wind up Jack Wilshire. It was a mad feeling to be a Tottenham fan who showed no fear of whoever we played and there was a swagger and a confidence, not just as a fan but to the football we were being treated to.

The thought that if we had postponed our move out of N17 and kept White Hart Lane for just one more season does pop into my head from time to time. That move came at the wrong time for the club, or did the promise of success appear too quickly? Maybe we would have won the league if we'd stayed at home for one more year. It's hard to say, especially as Pep Guardiola had infused City with his methods by now and they had won the league with a record 100 points. We finished 3rd with 77 points, still a great total but down on that of the previous season.

It was another cracking campaign to be a part of and one full of individual accolades for Harry Kane again. He scored the most amount of goals in the calendar year of 2017, even outpacing the likes of Cristiano Ronaldo and Lionel Messi. His partnership with Son was beginning to flourish and with Dele Alli and Eriksen behind him, the ammunition was just as great as the season before. It felt crucial though, that we had to win something, if not for ourselves but for this crop of players and Poch as we waited patiently to go back home.

2018/19 – Spurs are going back to Tottenham...and the Champions League final

The summer of 2018 was a strange one for us Spurs fans. We watched a large number of our players go deep into the World Cup in Russia, with Hugo Lloris lifting the Jules Rimet trophy and Harry Kane winning the Golden Boot. Our Belgian boys finished third as an England side made the semis for the first time in nearly thirty years. Things looked great and we were hoping that with this added experience our boys would be even hungrier for success on the domestic front at the start of the season.

You'd also think that our scouts were doing their utmost to add to a squad that was challenging on all fronts and yet, there were no transfers. Many stories have flown around since about why this was the case. With the new stadium still under construction and the purse strings tightened, had Daniel Levy told Mauricio Pochettino that he couldn't add to his side? Or was it true that Poch didn't want anybody? Whatever it was, before our opening day victory away to Newcastle, it was odd to see the same faces as last term with no new ones.

"Yeah, give it another week, lads." Tottenham Hotspur Stadium, summer 2018

Yet we made a brilliant start to the campaign with three wins out of three, the highlight being a 3-0 thrashing of Manchester United at Old Trafford, as Lucas Moura scored twice and showing exactly why we had purchased him back in January. But two back-to-back defeats against Watford and Liverpool brought us back down to Earth. Our Champions League form was truly awful in a "group of death" with Barcelona, PSV and Inter Milan. After an away defeat to the Italian side and a 4-2 demolition at Wembley at the feet of Lionel Messi and Barca, we had one point from three games and it looked impossible for us to escape the group. Yet, somehow we did! A late goal from Kane saw us come back to win 2-1 at home to PSV then we got revenge on Inter with a Christian Eriksen goal ten minutes from time. Then, in a nervy game at the Nou Camp, a Lucas tap-in drew us level against the mighty Barcelona and after hearing the result in the other game, the fans celebrations up in the gods broke the news to the players. We'd done it, into the knockout stages we went and I'd down most of a bottle of Jack Daniels just to get through that game!

By Christmas we sat second in the league, having lost four times but winning 15, including a 3-1 job on our old rivals Chelsea. Some of our football at the time was electric. On the 23rd December, I travelled up to Goodison Park with my soon-to-be Father-In-Law Gary to watch us take on his beloved Everton. I knew that I'd have to be on my best behaviour because I was in the Bullens with the home support. How would I hide my emotions from a bunch of scousers who were probably wondering why this Southern softy was sitting with them? In the end, I didn't have to worry because, despite an early wobble, we ran out 6-2 winners, thrashing the Toffees. I had to laugh really and was probably doing a bad job of containing my amusement. When Eriksen scored our fourth, a sumptuous half-volley from the edge of the area, I jumped up forgetting where I was for the moment but luckily, I regained my composure. By the time Sonny added a sixth poor Gary turned to me and said, "Hayden. I'm not bringing you again." Queue a nervous laugh, followed by a message telling me that my sister had gone into labour with my nephew. Freddie was born on Christmas Eve and with his parents being die-hard Spurs fans it wasn't long before he was wearing the kit!

My view from the Bullens, Goodison Park, as a secret away fan, December 2018

Then after the festive period, it all started to go a little sour. Sure, the football still looked good, but with the stadium being delayed maybe the players were starting to get a little fatigued of Wembley? Surely there would be some recruits in the January transfer window to freshen things up? Defeats to Wolves and Manchester United showed that we needed some new ideas as the title challenge slipped to Liverpool and Manchester City who were starting to extend their leads into a two-horse race. Then Poch started talking about the need for a "painful rebuild", having the right furniture for the new house and deflecting questions about the vacant manager's job at Real Madrid. But once again no one arrived and as the transfer window slammed shut, I was confident we'd get top four again and hopefully a trophy, despite going out on penalties to Chelsea in the League Cup semi-final not long after.

Luckily, as Harry Kane entered a period on the sidelines, Sonny picked up the mantle and crucial goals in three wins against Watford, Newcastle and Leicester kept us on track whilst in Europe we played one of our greatest-ever matches as we beat Borussia Dortmund 3-0 in our last European game at Wembley. The return to N17 was in touching distance but before then the returning Kane struck against the Scum in a match where Hugo Lloris salvaged a point with a last-minute penalty save that ultimately saw us finishing fourth at the end of the season and the Gooners finishing a point behind us. Lol.

But this all came in the middle of a five-game winless streak. A 2-1 loss at Burnley saw Poch publicly argue with referee Mike Dean, who had riled him into saying something he shouldn't have done. It seemed that the usually unflappable manager was starting to feel the strain and the squad looked shot. It wasn't helped by the January sale of Mousa Dembele and with Victor Wanyama struggling with injuries the midfield unit that had been so great was no more. By the time our first game in the Tottenham Hotspur Stadium came around in April, my confidence that we'd beat whoever we faced had all but gone. But in our amazing new home Son and Eriksen put Crystal Palace to the sword.

Ten days later, it was my first trip to the new gaff and I found it truly overwhelming. It was odd settling back into my matchday routine, but seeing this huge new impressive structure where the stadium I loved used to be. It was like a spaceship had landed there. I took it all in. I bought my beer that was filled from the bottom of the cup. I took and recorded so many photos and videos and FaceTimed family members and friends to show off just how impressive it all was. The day was completed by a brilliant 4-0 win over Huddersfield, where a weakened side was helped home by a Lucas hat-trick and a Wanyama strike. The stadium blew me away and yet, I didn't feel at home anymore. This was something new, something different and my Dad wasn't there with me. I couldn't tell him what I thought or ask him for his opinions. So after that game, I told myself it would be better if I went again with my children someday and not to go again on my own. As I was getting married that August, maybe the kids wouldn't be far off.

Back then and while our domestic form was a cause for concern our European one was cause for all-out celebration. Having disposed of Dortmund, we met Manchester City in the quarter-finals. Kane went off injured in the home tie so Sonny stepped up again to score and we took a slender 1-0 win to the Etihad. I sweated so much during those two games. The drama was almost too much and yet we eventually saw them off in a classic game at the Etihad. Then as we were drawn against Ajax in the semis, I allowed myself to dream. Maybe Tottenham could win the Champions League? Imagine that. It would be like Football Manager coming true!

The first Ajax game was a reminder of just how poor we had become. It was heartbreaking to watch but it did look like this fine Spurs side, the best of my lifetime, was coming to an end. Some favourites looked as though they were starting to wane and others, such as Kane, Wanyama and Rose, integral parts in the machine, had spent lots of time on the treatment table and were missing in parts of the season at crucial moments.

Hello darkness, my old friend. After the Ajax first leg. 2019

Thank God for Lucas Moura. The only Spurs player who was namechecked in my Groom's speech and for good reason. His hat-trick in the second leg against the Dutch champions saw us reach the Champions League final. It was a dream come true. I laughed, I cried, I pinched myself numerous times. That team I started supporting as a boy, the one that had underachieved time and time again and been the ridicule of so many now had the chance to become European champions.

Before that, we cemented our place back in the competition the following season with a 2-2 draw against Everton on the last day of the season meaning no matter what, we'd be there again next year. Then we had three weeks to wait...and wait...and wait...for the biggest game of our lives.

Who knows whether Harry Kane was fit or not for that final and whether Lucas should have played considering what he did in us getting there but the 2018-19 season, for all that was good about it, ended on such a heartbreaking note. Despite that, I can look back now on a special time and appreciate it for what it was. The last push of the best Tottenham side I have ever seen, managed by the best manager we've had in my time watching Spurs, almost achieved the unthinkable.

I wouldn't have missed it for the world.

Back home, first game at the Tottenham Hotspur Stadium against Huddersfield, 2019

2021-22 – Sonny's golden boot shines as we are back among the European elite

In November 2021, no one thought that Tottenham Hotspur would find themselves back in the Champions League at the end of the season. It just seemed so farfetched. Sitting tenth after ten games, having won five and lost five in the league and coming off a humbling defeat at home to Manchester United, a difficult summer for the club looked like it was going to stretch into a difficult winter too. New manager Nuno Espirito Santo's brand of football was at odds with that which the fans wanted, even what Daniel Levy had promised us that summer in wanting attacking football back in

N17 after the Josè Mourinho experiment. We'd also suffered the potential heartache of losing Harry Kane.

After several years of being the best player at the club, our homegrown legend had finally had enough of the lack of silverware and it was clear to everyone that the club was slipping down the table. Two years ago they were in the Champions League final, now they were taking part in the Europa Conference League, a new but by far inferior tournament and with Man City wanting him, Kane wanted out. He barely featured in pre-season but the club would not relent. He missed the opening day victory over his wannabe club and not long after threw in the towel and announced he would be staying for the season. But he was well off the pace until the festive period when Santo's short reign had thankfully ended.

The club had undergone an overhaul. Now we had a Football Director in the form of former Juventus man Fabio Paratici, who'd used his vast contacts to bring in Cristian Romero, Emerson Royale, Pierluigi Gollini, Bryan Gill and Pape Matar Sarr. The painful rebuild that Mauricio Pochettino warned about was in full swing but that November, we were managerless again and well off the pace of the front runners. We needed someone to galvanise a fractured squad. What we got was someone who we would never have predicted would be a Spurs manager one day.

Former Chelsea boss Antonio Conte arrived and I was stunned. My memory of the Chelsea side that he managed to the Premier League and the FA Cup was that they were dogged, pragmatic and counter-attacking, much like the way that Josè Mourinho liked his teams to play. I wasn't sold on his appointment. With a reputation of being a volatile character, was this the best person to lead a team like ours? We all knew he'd blow up the club at some point and set fire to his bridges when he eventually left. Was Daniel Levy sure that Conte was his man?

And this is why this season makes it into this list. Because when it worked under Conte, in this season, indeed only this season, it was brilliant. I also had a new Father glow in 2021 as our son, William, was born just before the lockdown was lifted in March. I'd also taken him as a young six-month-old and my Mum to the new Tottenham Hotspur Stadium for a tour, one in which we ended up bumping into Gary Mabbutt! So some of that old impetus that had left me after the crushing disappointment of 2019 was starting to return, just as Spurs were too.

Although our trek in the Conference League didn't come to anything after we were kicked out for having to postpone a match due to COVID, we went on a nine-match unbeaten run, taking in a 2-2 draw with Liverpool which saw Kane score his first league goal of the season, just six days before Christmas, and one we probably should have won. Yet it was the last match in that sequence that showed everyone that Spurs did have a winning mentality.

With 90+5 minutes on the clock, it looked like we were going to succumb to our first defeat under the Italian to Leicester. But when Steven Bergwijn equalised, I felt relieved that no "banter" would be coming my way that night. Then Tielemens gave the ball away from kick-off and it reached Kane, who played an inch-perfect through ball to Bergwijn who slipped the ball past Kasper Schmeichel and into the back of the net. We'd snatched victory from the jaws of defeat in an incredible end to the game that had me nearly waking the baby up with my celebrations!

There were still some frustrating results, such as a three-match losing streak that saw us lose to Chelsea, Southampton and Wolves. I was so despondent again that I didn't want to know how we'd get on against Man City at the Etihad. Luckily, I had a distraction in the form of my wife's 30th birthday dinner party. But the good old BBC Sport app kept me informed and an inspired performance from Harry Kane saw us score yet again in the 95th minute to win 3-2 in a match that January window signings from Juventus,(Dejan Kulusevski, who scored the opener, and Rodrigo Bentancur) excelled. The season had turned a corner again. Perhaps Champions League qualification wasn't too far off after all?

Then the inevitable meltdown from Conte nearly threw everything back into the skip. His moaning in his post-match interview of a dismal 1-0 defeat at Burnley was churlish as the Italian tried to save face, even suggesting he might not be the best person for the job. It was maddening but it affected his new side, who only lost twice more in the league from February onwards. Thrashings were dealt out to Everton, Leeds and Newcastle, not to mention the Scum in a game that was rescheduled to be played in the penultimate week of the season after they had the original fixture postponed because of one case of COVID in their squad.

The final day came and we had to match the Gooners score (how many times have we had to do this in the PL era?!) to finish above them and they had to pray that we'd lose away to relegated club Norwich. Even a case of food poisoning the week building up to the game, giving us lasagne gate levels of nerves again, didn't hold us up as we thrashed Norwich 5-0. Beating our rivals to the post felt so good. For the first time in three years, we'd be back in the Champions League and Sonny was the Golden Boot winner, having to share it with Liverpool's Mohammad Salah. The summer came and there was no talk of Kane wanting to leave plus in Sonny, we'd seen that he could be our main man even in the absence of the England captain. It felt good again to be a Spurs fan.

My son, William, aged six months, gets jammy and meets Gary Mabbutt, 2021

Honourable mention: 2023-24 – I'm loving Big Ange instead

Remember what I said about Conte blowing the club up before he left? Well, after he did that, the writing was on the wall for Daniel Levy. Towards the end of the 2022-23 season fans, had finally lost their patience with a man who had rebuilt the club but whose on-pitch success had brought only one trophy in twenty-two years. We were all unhappy and to add to that unhappiness corners of the German media were tapping up Harry Kane, linking him to Bayern Munich. Levy had to get it right that summer. This time, we needed a manager who could bring together a split fanbase and a disenchanted dressing room. Enter Ange Postecoglou.

The former Celtic manager had just won the treble up in Scotland, now he was the latest in a long line of managers hoping to bring success back to N17. Unlike his predecessor, Ange displayed a more approachable manner when it came to the players, but could still be prickly with the press. He was known for bringing an uncompromising attacking philosophy wherever he worked and that was just what we needed.

There was a clean sweep in the squad too. Throughout the season, the likes of Hugo Lloris and Eric Dier – club servants who had served the club well but were well past their expiry date with us – left for pastures new. In came Italian stopper, Guglielmo Vicario, as our new number one, Micky Van de Ven from Wolfsburg, James Maddison and Brennan Johnsen in a new-look and younger line-up. Just two days before the season started, Harry Kane's stay at Tottenham ended as he made the long-mooted move to Bayern. Fans were crestfallen, the love affair with our greatest-ever striker was over. Now it was up to Son, in his new role as club captain, to be our main talisman.

How good was the start to that season? After ten games in the league, we were top, having won eight and drawn two. The boys were playing a brand of expansive football that was thrilling pundits and other fans alike. We were forming a relationship with Ange too, who thanks to a reworded rendition of Robbie Williams's anthem "Angels", had the whole stadium serenading it to him after every game. Even the singer himself uploaded a post of him singing the new words on social media and declaring that he was a Spurs fan now.

The new boys had clicked, and we were winning well, including a memorable late show against Sheffield United and Liverpool, the latter a hilarious debacle that resulted in a VAR mistake, two sendings off and a comedy own goal at the end to give us all three points. Even Jürgen Klopp was crying about wanting a replay because the decisions were so bad. Oh yeah, Jürgen? Shall we replay the Champions League final then, eh?

Inevitably with us, it was all going to go wrong at some point and of course, it had to be Chelsea who ruined our season again. In a season-defining game which saw Romero and Destiny Udogie sent off, we finally succumbed to an onslaught after playing an ambitious high line and being caught out three times to lose 4-1. But Sonny had a goal chalked off when we were 1-0 up by VAR, Maddison and Van de Ven both went off with long-term injuries and all of a sudden, we looked dead again. After four defeats and one memorable 3-3 draw up at Manchester City when our defence consisted of four wing-backs, we finally got back up and running with a 4-1 win over rivals for Europe in the form of Newcastle. Richarlison came to the fore with a brace and went on a run of 11 goals in ten games. Since his move from Everton a year earlier for £60m, the Brazilian had only scored three goals in the previous campaign. After bravely opening up on the struggles in his personal life, the striker looked reborn as he filled in for Sonny, who like Pape Matar Sarr and Yves Bissouma, left for a month to represent their countries in major tournaments.

  The squad was further boosted by the purchases of Timo Werner on loan for the season and Radu Dragusin from Genoa as Dier's replacement, who joined Kane in Munich. We were scoring and conceding goals for fun. It was like a team with Poch's attack and Ardiles' defensive tactics on the same side! However, as our best players began to return, we started conceding a lot of set-piece goals, mainly from opposition players harassing Vicario, who otherwise was having an incredible first season with us. Ange was stubborn in press conferences, saying he didn't see any problem, which had us fans scratching our heads.

  With ten games to go, we were looking set for 4th place, especially after thrashing our nearest rivals for the coveted spot, Aston Villa, 4-0 at Villa Park in what was quite possibly the performance of the season. I was also basking in the glow of becoming a parent again as my daughter, Isabelle, had been born in February so all looked rosy going into the final push of the season. Sure, Ange had thrown the League Cup under the bus and we were unlucky in drawing Manchester City in the FA Cup 4th round, resulting in the Blues first win at the Tottenham Hotspur Stadium, but otherwise everything else looked good.

The warning signs came when we lost 3-0 away to Fulham but we put it down as a one-off. Then to round the season out we lost five out of the last seven games, only picking up maximums against relegated sides Burnley and Sheffield United. We were thrashed for the second consecutive season at St James' Park, this time a more humbling 4-0, then the title-chasing Gooners did us in our backyard 3-2, and we'd been 3-0 down at half-time in a game that saw a Van de Ven goal chalked off by VAR when we had been by far the better team. Worse was to come, when in desperate need of points to finish 4th, our game in hand over Villa came in the form of a home game against Man City. They were trailing our bitter rivals and needed two wins from their final two games to stop the Scum from winning their first title in twenty years.

From a fans' perspective, you don't want to see your team ever lose, but there is no possible way I wanted us to help the lot from South London to win the title. We'd never hear the last of it. Ange said in the build-up that it was just another game but after the 2-0 defeat, in which Sonny had been one-on-one late on to equalise and practically hand the title to the Gooners but missed, our normally composed boss was fuming. He claimed that people inside the club wanted to lose and that it stank of a poor mentality. The players wanted to win, they played so well that game and yet Ange had turned on a fan behind him during the game and then questioned us afterwards. It was a badly judged take from the Aussie manager, who later went back on it but once again it left fans open to ridicule and hate from rival fans. Still, those Gooner salty tears tasted good.

We finished 5th, far exceeding our expectations at the start of the year and despite how it all ended, I'm hoping that next season will build on this and that finally, surely, we get our name on some silverware...

2

BEST PLAYERS

Klinsmann, Sheringham, Keane, Alderwiereld, Lennon...just some of the names to miss out on my top eleven players in the Premier League era. Before you go off in a huff and burn this book, or flush it down a toilet, feast your eyes on the sheer talent that did make the list. And really, how we have won so little with them in the side is downright criminal...

Harry Kane - 2011-2023
Club Appearances: 435
Club Goals: 280

If I could go back in time and tell my younger self that the hapless-looking young striker who tripped over his boots in the friendly against Schalke and was laughed at by the crowd would end up our club's top goalscorer, he'd laugh in my face. He'd probably fall over if I then continued to tell him that he'd also become England's record goal scorer and yet, didn't Harry Kane prove us all wrong?

Kane's greatest strength, aside from his amazing ability to finish, was proving people wrong. People said he'd be a one-season wonder. He went on to win three Golden Boot awards in the Premier League. He also won the Golden Boot in the World Cup in Russia in 2018 and what made it sweeter was that Harry was one of our own. With individual honours too numerous to mention in this short section, it was a blessing to see him play multiple times live and with a few years left in the tank yet, surely he'll be back to add to his 213 Premier League goals and to hunt down Alan Shearer's record.

His multiple goals over the Scum make him the highest scorer in the North London derby and will always be my favourites, especially the incredible one when he ripped his mask off in celebration. Year after year he did it for us, forging a fantastic partnership with Son Heung-Min and after Christian Eriksen's departure he became, not just our best striker, but also our best playmaker.

For years we worried about losing him and when it finally happened, it hurt. We gave Harry the chance to lead us to glory and he almost led us to silverware too but a poor record in finals, and the fact that he still hasn't won anything at his new club, Bayern Munich, still makes him fair game to rivals' fans for mockery. We still love you Harry and I'm still crossing my fingers that he'll be back in our colours before he hangs up his boots to hopefully, finally, win something with us.

Son-Heung Min - 2015 - present
Club Appearances: 408
Club Goals: 162

When the South Korean superstar signed for us from Hamburg for £22 million in 2015, many fans saw the transfer as a cynical ploy for a boost in the club's profile in the Far East. What we ended up getting was one of the most popular, skillful, brilliant finishers the Premier League has ever seen. Yet, it didn't start too well for Sonny, as after a barren first season the forward had asked Mauricio Pochettino if he could leave. Luckily, he stayed and played his way into the side and into sensational form in a season where we finished second.

It just kept getting better and better from there. Before long, Son was banging in goals left, right and centre, with his devastating pace and ability to shoot from distance and always stepped up when his strike partner Harry Kane was injured.

But it isn't just the fact that the highest Asian goal scorer in the Premier League is a world-class player, he's also a bloody nice guy. Ask anyone who supports another club who they like most from our mob and I guarantee you that Sonny is the one they pick and who they probably dread coming up against most on matchdays.

Now one of our all-time greats, Son has also assumed club captaincy under Ange Postecoglou and it is a rich reward for a player who has given us great service and memories. His powerful run from box to box to slot home past Burnley in 2020 won the Puskás Award for best goal that season and I hope, like all of you, to see Sonny be the man who lifts some silverware for us before his career at Tottenham is over.

**Dele Alli - 2015 - 2022
Club Appearances: 269
Club Goals: 67**

When a teenage Dele Alli was scouted by former boss David Pleat and recommended to Spurs, we snapped him up for a cool £5m from MK Dons despite none of us knowing what impact he'd have on our club. Sure, he looked cheeky, with his wave to Sky Sports' cameras becoming an early indicator that we'd signed a fella with character. What we also discovered was that we had unearthed a supreme talent, one who with no hesitation in making him a club legend.

By the time he had turned 21, Dele had more goals than Paul Scholes, Steven Gerrard and Frank Lampard at the same age. He'd represented England at two major tournaments, taken part in two title challenges at Spurs and inDele-bly written himself into our hearts. His goals against Crystal Palace and the six he got over Chelsea in four memorable games sit well in my memory alongside him shushing the Stamford Bridge crowd. He took on Real Madrid and scored twice and was truly a generational talent.

There would be no Ajax memories if Dele hadn't of been so brilliant in that game, setting up two of Lucas' goals. He had the temperament and ability to have it all and yet, sadly, it wasn't meant to be.

What a shame that by the turn of the decade his magic had waned to such an extent that after a brief time in Antonio Conte's side, he was off to Everton. When we learnt of the reasons for his lack of form and the issues he was dealing with, it only made us more protective of Dele and even now I'd have him back in our squad in a heartbeat.

Come home Dele.

Gareth Bale - 2007-2013, 2020-21
Club Appearances: 237
Club Goals: 71

Bale's career with Spurs can be split into two categories. Not just because he came back to us, that'd be a lazy comparison, but think of the teenager with the hair clip and his fragile ankles and then fast forward six years to the physical specimen winning games on his own and staking a serious claim as one of the best players in the world.

When he arrived in N17 from Southampton in 2007 all I knew of him was that he had a wand of a left foot, was a month younger than me and that he was Welsh. He showed glimpses in his first season of what he'd become but injury did for him as did a horrendous track record of not being on the winning side for us for 24 league matches – covering three seasons! As soon as he was up and running, however, Bale found form and regular game time in the tail end of 2009-10 and goals in important wins against Arsenal and Chelsea saw us on the way to qualify for the Champions League, where our Welsh wizard found his place on the world stage.

We'll never forget his performances against Inter Milan in that incredible run. Nor his fantastic goals against Stoke, West Ham, Southampton and Sunderland that helped us get to our then-record points total in the league. With Bale picking up the PFA Young Player of the Year twice and Player of the Year in the 2013 season, when he scored 21 goals for us, it was clear that the biggest names in football would be after him and we couldn't keep the wolves at the door for long.

It was terrible when he finally left for a world record £85m to Real Madrid but when he arrived back on loan in 2020 I was one of those checking and refreshing my Twitter feed all day. A boyish vigour came over me when I saw him in his white people carrier entering Hotspur Way. I couldn't believe it when he was back on our side, helping himself to 16 goals in all competitions despite Josè Mourinho's best attempts to not play him. I wish he'd stayed another year but alas, Bale retired a year later, forever a legend and forever one of my all-time favourite players.

Ledley King – 1999-2012
Club Appearances: 323
Club Goals: 14

"This is my Club, my one and only Club."

There have been many who have come and gone before and since but Ledley truly is the King of White Hart Lane. Revered worldwide for his defensive capabilities (Thierry Henry once said he was the toughest player he came up against), our one club man and last captain to lift a major trophy will always hold such a special place for us Spurs fans. The first recipient of a mural outside the Tottenham Hotspur Stadium, Ledley wasn't just a great defender. He was a cool head, a composed footballer who fought through the pain barrier just to play for us.

When he first established himself as a first-team regular in the early 2000s it was a turbulent time at the club. Our previous captain had mutinied and left to join that lot down the road, and we'd just changed owners. Yet King was a young, steady anchor in a team trying to escape the mid-table mire and I sang "We've got Ledley at the back" to my heart's content every time I graced White Hart Lane. It was a reassurance when he played, but sadly, as time progressed, his playing time began to shrink.

Our England International should have got more caps and more appearances for us had it not been for his dodgy knee. An injury which meant he didn't train in the week and that he couldn't play two games in seven days. Watching him collect the League Cup in 2008, having played extra time too, you can tell how uncomfortable he felt. It must have been awful for him and eventually, his career cruelly came to an end in 2012.

But what memories did he leave us with? His goal against Bradford after 10 seconds – a Premier League record for years – his bullet header against the Scum, that incredible recovery tackle on Arjen Robben when the flying Dutchman was clean through on goal. His performance against France in Euro 2004. Leading us out in the Champions League for the very first time in the club's history (I know we were in the European Cup in 1961-62, but this was very new territory fifty years later) and generally being our stalwart. His testimonial was the most fun I've ever had at a game, too.

Forever King of the Lane.

Christian Eriksen – 2013-2020
Club Appearances: 305
Club Goals: 69

Who'd have thought that in a summer of signings that included Paulinho and Roberto Soldado that it was Eriksen's acquisition from Ajax that would turn out to be the bargain? Well, anyone who'd seen him play, that's who. Our £11.5 million Danish playmaker was an immediate success and turned out to be arguably the best creative midfielder we've had in the Premier League era. 88 assists is a truly impressive and the amazing cross to find Dele in the FA Cup semi-final against Chelsea sums up the sheer technique and qualities that made Eriksen so special.

Our favourite Dane wasn't just an assist machine. He was also a goal scorer of some truly sublime goals. Not afraid to take a punt from long range, Eriksen was also a brilliant free-kick specialist. His two dead ball strikes against Swansea and the 30-yarder against Sheffield United in the League Cup semi-final come immediately to mind, as does his first goal for the club in the league against West Brom. Amazing to think that with such pin-point accuracy how bad he was at taking corners and beating the first man!

That aside, when Eriksen was on song, so were we. The goals in successive seasons at the Bridge against Chelsea, the strike within ten seconds at Wembley against Manchester United, his last-minute winners against Burnley, Swansea, Brighton and Bournemouth showed just how important he was to us and how vital his goal contributions were.

It was a sad day when he left us for Inter Milan in the January transfer window in 2020. In need of a change, we watched the All or Nothing Amazon documentary as he sat with Daniel Levy and Josè Mourinho saying that he wanted to leave and he left a hole in our side for seasons to come. Not until the recent signing of James Maddison, have we had a midfielder who was fit to lace Eriksen's boots, let alone be mentioned in the same breath. And despite him turning out for Man Utd in recent years, it's a miracle he's still with us after his on-field cardiac arrest during Euro 2020. A special talent, a special player and one who is always welcome back in N17.

Hugo Lloris - 2012-2023
Club Appearances: 447
Club Goals: 0

Much maligned considering how his Tottenham career went in the end but at one point it wasn't an exaggeration to say that we had one of the best goalkeepers in the world in Hugo. The French stopper, who is his country's most capped player with 145 appearances, kept 151 clean sheets in 12 seasons and captained us in the time that we transformed into title challengers.

When he first arrived in 2012, our new sweeper keeper had to wait a few months to displace Brad

Friedel to become our undisputed number one but once it was his, no one else came close to filling his place between the sticks. With a catalogue of unbelievable saves – his goal line grab against Bayer Leverkusen in the Champions League still beggars' belief – Lloris was one of our most outstanding players in a team that looked like it was going places.

He was also handy in a penalty situation, famously saving against Pierre-Emerick Aubameyang in the final minute of a crucial North London Derby and denying Sergio Aguero in the first leg of our famous European campaign in 2019. He led the side admirably and was so cruelly denied the chance to win anything with us.

Then, sadly, after 2019, our Hugo became a shadow of his former self. After he dislocated his elbow in a sickening injury whilst conceding at Brighton, it looked like our skipper's number had been called. But an Indian summer under Antonio Conte saw Lloris earn a reprieve after injury and form had started to tank. Sadly, though, his 447th appearance in the 6-1 capitulation away to Newcastle in 2023 was his last. After conceding five goals in 20 minutes, whatever the Frenchman said in the dressing room at half-time meant that he never wore our colours again. An undignified end to such a great club servant.

Jan Vertonghen – 2012-2020
Club Appearances: 315
Club Goals: 12

When it comes to defenders, few were as classy, consistent and dependable as Super Jan. A £9.5 million signing from Ajax, Vertonghen stepped into the void that recently retired Ledley King left in our defence and right from the word go he looked a class apart. In a debut Premier League season, he managed six goals in 46 appearances and was even voted in the Premier League Team of the Year. With his stock sky high, it looked like the future was bright for our Belgian International.

For the next couple of seasons, Vertonghen suffered injury, a drop off in form and lost his consistency much in the way that the team did but found his feet again when Mauricio Pochettino joined. He formed a brilliant partnership with compatriot and friend Toby Alderweireld, helping us to concede just 26 goals in the entire league campaign in 2016-17.

Individual performances stand out against Borussia Dortmund in the Champions League round of 16 in 2019, when Super Jan, playing at left-back, was Man of the Match in a game that saw him lay one on a plate for Sonny then thump one in himself, leading to his trademark celebration of ripping his shirt like Superman. His last-minute winner away to Wolves in 2019 also lives long in the memory at a time when his career with us looked like it was coming to an end.

Following an accidental collision with Alderweireld the previous season, Vertonghen's performances were tailing off and with the defender now hitting his mid-thirties, the club decided to let him go at the end of his contract. The look of abject disappointment after being substituted in an FA Cup tie against Norwich told us that even he knew he was coming to the end.

However, Super Jan has rebuilt his career at Benfica and Anderlecht, even becoming Belgium's all-time most-capped player in the process. It was later revealed that the collision with Alderweireld had resulted in months of headaches and dizzy spells for Vertonghen, hampering his performances with us in the process. We were deprived of a proper send-off for the legend during the COVID crisis and it's a shame that such an innocuous moment led to a premature end for one of the best defenders I've seen at the Lane.

Jermain Defoe – 2004-2008, 2009-2014
Club Appearances: 362
Club Goals: 143

In an era when the club was dripping in striking talent, no one in my view was a more deadly finisher than JD. A January transfer signing for a snip at £7 million. In Defoe, not only had we poached arguably the best striker outside of the top flight, but he was also one of the best young talents this country had produced and went on to become our fifth (at the time) top goal scorer and our most prolific scorer in Europe (until a certain Mr Harry Kane came along).

In his first spell, he was instrumental in helping rebuild the club in challenging for European contention again. Under Martin Jol, he was our best player in 2004-05, scoring a hat-trick against Southampton along the way and a brilliant goal against the Scum. The following season he lost out to Mido and Robbie Keane and even lost a place in the England squad for the World Cup in 2006. His hunger to regain his place in the Spurs and national side saw him take every opportunity possible but eventually, as Keane formed a brilliant partnership with Dimitar Berbatov, Defoe took his leave just before we won the Carling Cup in 2008 with 64 goals to his name for Portsmouth and first-team football.

Fast forward six months and he was back and undeniably for two seasons our best striker again. In the run-up to our qualification for the Champions League for the first time, Defoe was our highest scorer and equalled a five-goal haul record in the League in an incredible 9-1 win over Wigan Athletic.

Before long JD was a centurion, bringing up 100 goals for the club and although he started to play more of a bit part again behind Rafa Van der Vaart and Emmanuel Adebayor, we had Defoe during his best years. He was a Spur through and through and when he finished his career with us for good in 2014, carried shoulder high around White Hart Lane, it was a fond farewell to a club servant who is now back at the club as a coach with the youth team, hopefully passing down his talents to the legends of the future.

JD takes pity on my broken arm and signs my shirt. 2008

Luka Modrić – 2008-2012
Club Appearances: 160
Club Goals: 17

A bit of a retrospective one, this, as at the time – and I know this is a controversial take – I didn't rate Luka Modrić much. After joining us from Dinamo Zagreb for a record-equalling £16.5 million, he struggled in his first few months, though who didn't in that horrendous start to the 2008-09 season? After that, however, Modrić began to repay that big fee (for the time) and his mercurial talents helped us to gain Champions League qualification and then he signed a six-year deal to stay with the club.

Another season on and Chelsea was sniffing about and a £40 million bid was placed, which we flatly turned down. I couldn't understand why Modrić was so highly rated. This was a point where I was going to nearly every home game and the Croatian just didn't do it for me. I always thought that someone with his talent and vision should have been posting better numbers. The fact that in over a decade he's won countless titles and millions of Champions League trophies, The FIFA World Cup Golden Ball and been a Ballon d'Or winner shows really why you shouldn't listen to me about players!

Then I went back through the old season review DVDs and watched him again and it clicked. He was the conduit of which all that was good came through him. The metronome who kept the team on time. So what if he only made 3 or 4 assists a season? He was the one unpicking the lock for those around him.

Truly, one of the best footballers of all time, certainly Croatia's best, and he was ours for a few years.

Add to that his stunning goals against Liverpool and Bolton in his final season and the one he swept in against Chelsea to give us a 1-0 home win, and we had Modrić, like Bale, when his talents were just coming to the fore and those of us who were there to watch them were truly lucky.

Dimitar Berbatov – 2006-2008
Club Appearances: 102
Club Goals: 46

I had a bit of a man crush on Dimitar Berbatov. How could you not? With those smouldering eyes, the slicked-back dark hair and tall physique he was enough to make anyone question which side their bread was buttered. He's not in here for his looks, of course, and although he did just stay for two years, he has sneaked onto this list in front of other strikers like Robbie Keane, Jürgen Klinsmann and Teddy Sheringham for good reason. I felt that Dimitar Berbatov was the living embodiment of all that I had been taught was good about Tottenham Hotspur Football Club.

The flair, the doing things with style, one of the most naturally gifted footballers of his generation. If you could build an ultimate Tottenham player at the time, it was Berbatov. My Dad and Grandad used to say this all the time when they would regale me with their stories of days gone by and the attributes Berba was gifted with. The touch of Hoddle, the finishing of

Greaves, the strength of Bobby Smith the movement of Gilzean, the arrogance and panache of Ginola and the moodiness of Steve Archibald, Berbatov was the ultimate striker and he knew it.

Take his penalty in the Carling Cup final. The calmest man in Wembley, nae every pub and bar across the world watching that game, Berba tip-toed up and rolled the ball home like he was kicking into an open goal in his garden. The approach typified the Bulgarian and in two years with us he was awesome. Like Hoddle before him, he had a knack for scoring great goals. The turn and run against Charlton from the halfway line. The volley from the edge of the area against Middlesborough. The mazy run in Besiktas. The tight finish against the Scum and then, of course, the four goals in the mad 6-4 home game against Wigan.

I was heartbroken when he left for Manchester United, and when he refused to sign an autograph for me at a friendly at Carrow Road, and for a while he was hated at White Hart Lane but time is a great healer and he's a welcome guest at the Tottenham Hotspur Stadium nowadays. Just look at the reception he got when we left the Lane and he was announced onto the pitch. One of the silkiest players ever and one I wish I still had my framed photo of so that I could sigh at it now and then.

Me, 18 and hungover on Christmas morning, opening my Berbatov photo frame, 2007.

My Best Tottenham Premier League Eleven

Hugo Lloris

Ledley King (c)   Toby Alderweireld   Jan Vertonghen

Christian Eriksen   Luka Modrić

Aaron Lennon   Dele   Gareth Bale

Harry Kane   Heung-Min Son

3

CULT HEROES

What makes a cult hero? A mercurial maverick who can take the game by the scruff of the neck? Someone who in the blink of an eye can produce something magical, but possibly not all the time? A player whose attributes aren't great but gives their all for the team and the fans love them for that? Someone who still wears their Spurs badge with pride long after they have left us and the love affair endures? A journeyman who has seen it all and gives us his final years? Someone who goes under the radar until they have left and then we fully appreciate what we've lost? I'd say it's all these things. In this chapter, you'll find players who would easily make anyone's greatest list to represent our great club and some who wouldn't but would make you smile when you remember them. I know I do.

David Ginola – 1997-2000
Club Appearances: 124
Club Goals: 22

In the deep dark recesses of the 1990s, one man stood alone in bringing flair and entertainment to the masses at White Hart Lane and that man was David Ginola. Having seen glimpses of his magic at Newcastle in a side that finished runners-up to

Manchester United two seasons in a row, we couldn't believe our luck when the 30-year-old signed for us in July 1997 for £2.5 million. And was he worth it? Boy, wasn't he just.

Despite playing in arguably our worst side that decade, Ginola's tricks and flicks dazzled the Tottenham turf. In his first season, we struggled for consistency and were almost relegated but everyone could see how special he was. Yet, with his good looks and A-star celebrity status, David thrived in North London and was a flower in a pot of dirt in those Christian Gross/George Graham years. And then, in 1998-99, he turned on the charm.

Ginola was truly head and shoulders above the rest, being nominated by his peers as the PFA Player's Player of the Year and the Football Writer's Player of the Year too, in a season dominated by United's treble success. Ginola had been integral in making sure that wasn't a quadruple when he set up two and scored one in our Worthington Cup quarter-final against them. Although he was marked out of the final against Leicester, he emerged a winner as we won and cemented his place as a hero. He was so close to helping us to the FA Cup final too, scoring two memorable and brilliant goals against Barnsley and Leeds and we loved him.

Sure, he was a luxury player and compared to what we have now I'm not so sure he'd put enough work in to make it as an icon at Spurs in this time, but he was extravagant and embodied everything that Tottenham is about; doing things in style. Graham, who never looked like he wanted to play him even though he was our best player at the time, finally offloaded him to Aston Villa but whenever he's been back at the Lane or the new stadium he's been welcomed as one of our own. There's a mutual love between Ginola and the club that cements his place on this list.

Paul Robinson – 2004-2008
Club Appearances: 175
Club Goals: 1

It takes a special kind of player to build up such goodwill with fans that we still love him even as his career with us begins to tank. Paul Robinson had been such a revelation when he joined us for £1 million from Leeds in the summer of 2004, mainly because he was an instant upgrade on Kasey Keller, but also because he brought with him a young, homegrown potential that could be nurtured. In a sense he was a bit of a trailblazer in that regard as after him we started recruiting more young English talent into our ranks and despite having been relegated with the Yorkshire club, it was so obvious that Robbo was the future for club and country and he was an instant hit.

It also helps if your form brings about a solidity in the defence that gave Spurs the perfect platform for the good that was to come in the Martin Jol years. How we loved singing, "England's number one" at him and how he loved us back. He'd even start terrace chants himself, singing, "Stand up if you hate A*****l," to get the away fans going before a UEFA Cup match against Slavia Prague. And so, Robbo's career for club and country began to soar.

True, his positioning was questionable from time to time. My abiding memory of Robbo was watching him dive like a man out of an exploding room as the likes of Tugay, Paul Scholes and William Gallas scored worldies against him, leading me to wish that he'd saved the bloody shot instead of pulling off another Hollywood dive.

Then there was the back pass that ruined his career. When Gary Neville passed him a bobbling ball on a very lumpy pitch that sailed over his swinging boot, Robbo's confidence took a beating at the hands of the press. Before long, he looked like a shadow of his former self in a season when we too were finding things difficult in the league. To see Robbo making so many mistakes after that, and being visibly upset that he'd made them, enduring him more to fans and after his crazy goal against Watford gave him even more cult status, it was only fitting that he was the man between the sticks when we beat Chelsea in the 2008 Carling Cup final.

Robbo's career never really recovered after his England howler though and in the time in which he should have been hitting his peak, we sold him to Blackburn where he would end up being relegated and never reclaiming his England place. We still loved him and his visible emotion when the fans sang his old chant at the Farewell to White Hart Lane ceremony was touching. You'll always be England's number one to us.

Rafael Van der Vaart – 2010-2012
Club Appearances: 77
Club Goals: 28

When Harry Redknapp signed Rafael Van der Vaart for £8 million just after deadline day in 2010, Spurs fans couldn't believe our luck. A star for Real Madrid and Holland, the attacking midfielder's arrival was lauded as being up there with the purchases of Ardiles, Villa and Klinsmann. It was revolutionary that a team like Spurs, who had just achieved Champions League qualification for the first time, could attract a player of Van der Vaart's quality and with the Dutchman at his peak too.

It wasn't long before VDV's goals and passionate celebrations were endearing him to the White Hart Lane faithful. In his first full month at the club, he scored three goals in four games, formed a good partnership with Peter Crouch and won the Premier League Player of the Month. He also scored in five consecutive Premier League games, equalling a record shared by Teddy Sheringham and Robbie Keane.

Then, there were those full-blooded performances against the Scum which cemented VDV as a cult hero. He played like one of us out there. In every North London Derby he played in, he gave nothing less than everything he had to get one over on them and on occasion, thanks to him, we did. Who can forget him shushing the crowd after equalising in our win at the Emirates? Or repeating the feat in the home game later that season? The players had to stop him from being lost in the crowd when we beat them at home the following season. Rafa knew what it meant and for that, he was a legend.

Despite his fitness issues – he rarely completed 90 minutes and had hamstrings like biscuits – when VDV was there, he was a talisman for a side who were aiming for big things. Sadly, he only spent two-and-a-bit seasons at the club as Redknapp was sacked and AVB sent him off to Germany just two games into his reign but we will never forget the magic Rafa Van der Vaart brought to the club on those first Champions League nights and in that brilliant Harry Redknapp team.

Sandro – 2010-2014
Club Appearances: 106
Club Goals: 3

You'll be forgiven for thinking that I loved Sandro more than some of our best players in this next bit but I thought he'd go on and be our midfield enforcer for a decade. However, it didn't look promising for our young Brazilian midfielder when he made his debut in a derby against the Scum in 2010. The 21-year-old signing from Internacional was as lost as a little lamb in an abattoir but soon he became someone who we adored and a real pit bull in the middle of the park. Harry Redknapp likened his tenacious attitude to that of Dave Mackay, something that had us fans dribbling with anticipation that he would rip it up for us for many years to come. No wonder we used to call him "Beast."

A few months into his Spurs career, Sandro, alongside Wilson Palacios, put in an unbelievable performance at the San Siro as we beat Italian giants AC Milan 1-0. A long-range strike against Chelsea at Stamford Bridge did more to bring him into our collective bosom. Despite being a more defensive-minded player, Sandro also had a habit of scoring memorable goals. Another rocket against Manchester United and a wonderful effort against QPR helped increase his popularity at the Lane.

His online antics – being a proficient guitar player and frequenting his local pub to indulge in his new-found love for darts, added to his cult status. Fully embracing himself in our culture by learning Coldplay songs and being best mates with Bobby George puts Sandro up there as one of our zaniest players of the Premier League era.

And yet, what could have been? Forging a brilliant partnership with Moussa Dembele, his impact on the side was hampered by a serious knee injury that ruled him out for the rest of the season and poor Sandro was never the same after. By 2014 he was off to QPR and we were left to wonder what could have been.

Steffen Freund – 1998-2003
Club Appearances: 128
Club Goals: 0

If the ultimate cult hero could be defined in one player, that person would have been Steffen Freund. For four years he showed heart, commitment and never-say-die work ethic. He tried his best for us and bled for the side, a fact reaffirmed years later when he was spotted watching on from the stands with the fans before he became a coach in the AVB set-up.

On the face of it, Freund was a typical George Graham signing. He was a clogger; someone who could break up play in midfield and didn't get forward at all. In all his club appearances for us, he never scored once (barring one in an 8-1 friendly win over Stevenage Borough, but have you ever seen any footage to prove it?) and yet how we delighted in yelling "Shoot!" every time he was on the ball no matter where he was on the pitch. Then again, when he did take a punt, normally they'd hit the advertising boards in the upper tier, earning him the nickname "EasyJet" as they were the sponsors plastered all around the Lane back then.

In his first season, the former Borussia Dortmund and Germany International added a Worthington Cup winners medal to the Champions League he picked up two years prior and remained a fan favourite well into his final years with us, eventually being let go on a free by Glenn Hoddle at the end of the 2002-03 season.

On a day in which we'd been mullered by Blackburn 4-0, Freund upstaged even the farewell of the great Teddy Sheringham as the fans who stayed after the abysmal showing sang the, "I love Steffen Freund" song and serenaded the visibly touched German on the lap of honour. Sure, we've had better midfielders before and since but none of them were as fun to watch as your Freund and mine.

Mousa Dembele – 2012-2019
Club Appearances: 250
Club Goals: 10

If we had Mousa Dembele at his peak now, we'd be title challengers.

Another contender for the Best Players list in this book, Mousa Dembele's signing from Fulham in the summer of 2012, came with much promise. With Luka Modrić having ditched us for sunnier climes, the Belgian midfielder had recently put on a show against Manchester United at Old Trafford in a famous win for the Cottagers and looked like just the man to fill the Croatian's place in the middle of the park.

After he scored on his debut against Norwich, I was instantly taken to him. Indeed, I thought we would be getting a bit of a midfield goal machine in Dembele, considering he had started as a striker in his early days as a professional in Holland. Instead, Dembele struck up an awesome partnership with Sandro and with his skilful imposing frame was near impossible to shift off the ball.

Even when out of form and out of the team in the 2013-14 and 2014-15 seasons, I was calling out for my second favourite Belgian (sorry Mousa, but Super Jan takes first place) to be given a chance. By the time Mauricio Pochettino started utilising him more, we reaped the rewards and that player who most of his teammates would say was the best at the club began to show off his talents, riding challenges and going past people like they were not there.

Some people say that the slow rot of the Poch years started when Kyle Walker left for Manchester City but look at how our domestic campaign began to falter when Dembele left for China in January 2019. At the time we were title contenders and boy, how I would have loved to have had him in the Champions League final in Madrid but the Belgian's legs were starting to lose their speed. I still shed a tear when I think of his tweet excitedly declaring he couldn't wait to play at the Tottenham Hotspur Stadium. How cruel he never would play there.

Mousa, I miss you and I wish life was like Football Manager and we could sign your regen.

Moussa Sissoko – 2016-2021
Club Appearances: 202
Club Goals: 5

Here's a story of how hard work and determination can be the catalyst for changing fans' minds.

£30 million was a lot to spend on a player back in 2016, especially on one who had just been relegated from the Premier League and not a first-team regular, yet that is what we did with Moussa Sissoko. The former Newcastle midfielder was tall, imposing, and on occasion a little clumsy in his first season with the club and for a while looked like yet another expensive mistake by Daniel Levy. He struggled to break up the midfield pairing of Mousa Dembele and Victor Wanyama and never really looked at the races when he did make an appearance.

That all changed in 2017-18. With Wanyama beginning to miss game time with injury, slowly Sissoko found his way, not just in the Spurs side, but into the hearts of the Tottenham fans. By the end of the decade, his displays in Mauricio Pochettino's starting eleven had led him to gain a chant from the Spurs faithful (to the tune of The White Stripes' Seven Nation Army) a chant that was the first thing that his teammates started singing in the dressing room after our heroic Champions League win over Manchester City in 2019.

And so Sissoko became a cult figure, even winning the inaugural Tottenham Hotspur Legends' Player of the Season award before we clashed with Liverpool in the Champions League final. How cruel it was that it was his arm that the ball fell onto in the first minute of that game to rob him, and us, of a chance of glory.

Still, as highlighted in the All or Nothing series on Tottenham Hotspur, the Frenchman was held up as an example of how hard work can change a career. Just a pity his compatriot, Tanguy Ndombele, didn't follow his lead.

Lucas Moura – 2018-2023
Club Appearances: 221
Club Goals: 39

The figure at the centre of our greatest night in recent history, Lucas Moura, was a sound acquisition in the January transfer window in 2018. The lightning-fast Brazilian took some time to find his feet in the Premier League after moving from PSG but in the 2018-19 season he was unstoppable. So much of our early season form was punctuated by our latest signing (he was the last player we signed for the first team for 18 months), as he helped himself to a brace in the 3-0 win over Manchester United at Old Trafford. He then scored the all-important equaliser at the Nou Camp which saw us through to the Champions League knockout stages where his fate as a Spurs legend was waiting.

  His performance in that game is enough to allow Lucas into cult folklore. Needing three goals to go through to the final, the winger, in the absence of Harry Kane, stood up and put in a sensational performance that no one in love with the club will ever forget. His tears at the end matched ours. How sad it was to see him dropped for the final, even if it was understandable why he didn't start, with Kane now deemed fit.

  As the Poch years changed into our days under Josè Mourinho, Lucas kept his place in the side and continued with moments that punctuated his love for us and us in him. The first player to score a hat-trick in the new Tottenham Hotspur Stadium, his pinching of a fan's hat in the mad celebrations in the last minute against Leicester, being substituted off by Nuno Espirito Santo and the fan's boos seemingly helping to get the Portuguese manager sacked, his enthusiastic social media posts (COYS COYS COYS COYS COYS COYS) and his final ever goal for us, the mazzy dribble against Leeds United in his final kick. Lucas will be loved forever by our fans and if I ever meet him, I'll buy him a pint, shake his hand and thank him for Ajax.

Erik Lamela – 2013-2021
Club Appearances: 257
Club Goals: 37

A marmite player for many, Erik Lamela always failed to live up to some fan's expectations. As the supposed replacement for Gareth Bale, the £25.8 million signing from Roma struggled with injuries and form in his first season with the club but in early glimpses never really looked like holding a candle to the departed Welsh wizard.

All of that changed when Mauricio Pochettino took over. His Argentinian compatriot showed faith in Lamela and was rewarded with the sublime, his rabona goal in the Europa League plus his frequent displaying of the dark arts in football showed that our Erik was very much our shithouser too.

Despite this, I always thought that Lamela gave us all that he could. When he was in our colours he was great to watch. Sure, sometimes he could be infuriating – like when he took the ball from Sonny and missed a penalty against City when the South Korean was the spot-kick taker – and now and then he let his lack of discipline get the better of him. His memorable strikes against Manchester United ("LAMELLLLLAAAAAAAAAAAAAAAA!!!!!! One, two, three!", screamed commentator Martin Tyler) and the Scum, another rabona which won the

Puskás Award in 2021 live long in the memory and cement his place on this list.

Plus, anyone who winds up the Arse and calls Jack Wilshire a ****y is a hero in my book.

Roman Pavlyuchenko – 2008-2012
Club Appearances: 113
Club Goals: 42

When I was studying sports journalism at college there was one guy that me and my Spurs mates began to hero worship and that was Super Pav. The Russian stepped into the unenviable void left by the recently departed Dimitar Berbatov and Robbie Keane and into a side that was struggling at the wrong end of the table. Yet, it wasn't long before he'd won us over, his last-minute winner against Liverpool that season confirming his cult hero status in our eyes.

He's also the only Spurs player I've been genuinely starstruck by when meeting him in a club shop signing session in Harlow. I sang the Super Pav chant even if he wasn't playing. Some fans thought that Pav lacked the cutting or physical edge to make it in the Premier League but he posted an impressive goal return in his four years in N17. Not bad for a guy who wasn't a guaranteed starter under Harry Redknapp (who famously once gave him the tactical instruction, "Just run around a bit!" before coming on in a game once).

I'm convinced that Pavlyuchenko is one of the reasons why we qualified for Champions League football in 2010. He scored some really important goals in the run-up to the end of the season and when we were in Europe's elite competition, scored an important away goal in the qualifying round against Young Boys, then tapped in the third at home against Inter Milan.

He eventually left in 2012 after becoming frustrated with first-team opportunities but I for one would love to have a player of his calibre around the side now. Considering he was vying for a place against the likes of Keane, Darren Bent, Jermain Defoe, Peter Crouch, Rafa Van der Vaart and Emanuel Adebayor, 42 goals in 113 appearances is a more than decent return.

Edgar Davids – 2005-2007
Club Appearances: 44
Club Goals: 1

When the world-famous Edgar Davids signed for Spurs on a free transfer from Inter Milan in 2005 it sent a shockwave through the Gribble household. At 32 years of age, the Dutchman may have been past his peak but having someone with that amount of experience and tenacity in midfield alongside the sublime Michael Carrick was so exciting. I went a bit Davids mad. I bought a shirt with his name on it and printed out a photo of him in a Spurs kit to blu-tac against my wall. It was amazing to have such a famous superstar at the Lane. Here was someone who adorned the FIFA cover and who I signed frequently for my Spurs team on the game and now here he was playing for us!

Sure, he only stayed for just over a season but Pitbull was just the kind of player we needed to propel us up the table. Among a team of highly promising talents, he helped marshal us to 5th in the table and was one of those who played in our infamous final game at West Ham (in which he had a stinker, no pun intended). His only goal for us came against Wigan and it was a beauty. Come the start of the following season he lost his place to recruit Didier Zokora and went back to Holland but his presence left a mark on me.

Whether he qualifies as a bonafide Spurs legend is another conversation but he had been invited back for Ledley King's testimonial in 2014 and to the Farewell of White Hart Lane in 2017 and to my teenage self, Davids' arrival was my generation's Klinsmann moment. I know of a few people who sat glued to Sky Sports News eagerly awaiting confirmation that he'd passed his medical. Yes, I was one of them. In Davids, it proved that we had star-pulling power. It's crushing to think that I only saw him play twice in our colours (EMA money for sixth-form students didn't quite cover travel and matchday tickets back in the day).

No matter what your views on whether he's a proper legend for us, Davids's signing changed Tottenham, that's for certain.

4

BEST KITS

You can't reinvent the wheel, but you can bloody well give it a go. Yet, while our original all-white shirts of the 1960s remain the definitive Spurs shirt since sponsorship entered the fray in the mid-seventies, many have tried to emulate the original. From Umbro, Hummel, Puma, Pony, and Adidas to Nike and everyone else in between, there have been some absolute belters over the years. Here are my favourites...

1991-94 Umbro third kit

First up, we have this stupendous classic strip from Umbro which acted as our third kit in the early to mid-nineties. Sky blue with the word "SPURS" embroidered along the top of the front and back, it was classy, subtle and sleek and one of those that fans still like to look out for on eBay.

The design is similar to the one that England wore very rarely circa Italia 90 and so it has that certain 90s retro feeling. Plus, it has a collar, and I bloody love a collar on my kits. Very, very hazy memories of seeing Teddy Sheringham, Darren Anderton and Nick Barmby wearing it come to my mind when I think of it and of the replica shirts it's the one that I wear most. A behemoth in the pantheon of classic Spurs shirts.

2016-17 Under Armour home shirt

Some kits get on this list purely because they are associated with the good times. Others because they look great. This one falls somewhere in the middle for me. With the skin-tight white and navy design subtly trimmed with gold, it evokes the glory that we so nearly got that season, ending with a record 86 points and finishing second. It's iconic and brings back memories of the last days of White Hart Lane.

It was to be the last kit designed by Under Armour and it was undoubtedly the best they provided us. Even the inclusion of the navy blue on the shoulders and top of the shirt wasn't as gratuitous as some previous efforts. And when it appeared alongside the white shorts in Europe...*chefs kiss*

2004-05 Kappa away kit

I am smug to say that I was gifted this shirt as a teenager back in the day and I can still wear it now! This one is my running shirt nowadays (the 2002-03 navy shirt preceded it until it disintegrated in the wash!) This all-navy number is simple in design, look and feel. Indeed, all the kits that season only bore one colour (white, of course, for the home kit and yellow for the third kit) and the only Kappa kit that didn't feel like it was trying to strangle your body as you wore it.

It did become a second skin to me back in the mid-noughties as I used to wear this one under my black hoodie most weeks at sixth form and even on nights out. Looking back now, considering it was so snug and I was probably a very smelly teenager, I'm surprised this isn't the shirt that fell apart instead!

1999-2001 Adidas home kit

Whilst one of the Adidas kits from this era makes it onto my worst list (see Chapter 11 in the book for which one that is) the home kit in itself is arguably the best home kit we've had in the Premier League era.

Is the Holsten sponsor on the front? Check. Adidas stripes on the arms? Tick. No red whatsoever on the kit. That's another tick. A navy collar that said spurs on the back of it? Drools.

Sure, this was around the time that we were duller than dishwater to watch but whilst the football was Pony, thankfully, the Adidas design.

Kid sister Rohanna, wearing our other sister, Clara's old Holsten kit, 2009

1993-95 Umbro home kit

I was sorely tempted to include this kit's predecessor, which we wore in the 1991 FA Cup final, but with the yellow trim on the sleeves and collar of Umbro's final Tottenham home shirt, and the fact that it's the first home kit I can vividly remember, means that it holds a more special place in my heart. It's the shirt that Jürgen Klinsmann wore when he joined us from Monaco, the one we wore as we went to Anfield in the FA Cup quarter-final and beat Liverpool and so many early Spurs memories are tied to it.

It's the one so many of us wore as we dived across the grass, carpet or hall floor in salute to our German hero and in my mind, the best home kit of the era. It was also the last one before it all got a bit Pony and, like Klinsmann, we missed it when it was gone.

1991-95 yellow away kit

As I write this in 2024 there has been a renaissance of classic kits. Now they are seen as being better designed and cheaper than their modern-day counterparts, some of which are trying to emulate those that have gone before them. One, however, will never be copied again and that's this one. Why? Well, that splurge of bird poo on the shoulder would probably make it very meme-able.

Despite that part of the shirt, it remains one of our finest and most identifiable away kits in our history. Possibly because of its longevity (imagine shirt sponsors being brave enough to keep a strip the same for four years now) but also for its notoriety. It was made famous by Ronny Rosenthal's hat-trick against Southampton and Gary Lineker wore it too. I've even got a rare Powerpod of his knee sliding in it.

2007-08 Puma home and anniversary kit

The home kit, there's not much to say about it. All-white, no trim or thrills and no-nonsense. It also had a v-neck and Mansion red being the only smear on an otherwise brilliant shirt in a special commemorative year for our great club.

We wore it when we beat the Scum 5-1. We wore it the last time we won a trophy. We also took the pitch in this strip in those bonkers home matches against Reading and Chelsea but my enduring memory of this one was King Ledley and Keano holding a trophy aloft whilst wearing it.

But the one-off 125th half-and-half kit, commissioned for our birthday game in the equally baffling 4-4 home draw against Aston Villa, was also a work of art. The white/pale blue strip was a cash grab from the club, true, but it also symbolised where we had come from. No, not Blackburn. It's symbolic of the kit we wore in 1884 and boy did it look good, even if it were just for one game.

2001-02 Adidas home kit

Having already waxed lyrical about how much I loved the shirts from the early noughties, this one differed in several ways from its predecessor. The collar was gone, replaced with two shades of blue – one navy and one sky blue – in a v-collar design. The

Adidas stripes were still on the arms and rather symbolically, this was also the last time that our shirt sponsor wasn't red stained, with the Holsten logo adorning our kits for the final time.

It was with this shirt that I became a bit of a full kit w*****r. Yes, teenage me would wear the entire strip, shirt, shorts, the lot, all the time. Down the park when I played football with my mates, on school trips, to the games, you name it, I wore it then. Probably a good thing I outgrew it otherwise I'd be tempted to wear it to this day!

We battered Chelsea 5-1 in this one, and my memories of secretly wearing it under my school shirt the next day, flashing the badge at my Chelsea friends felt all kinds of sweet. Until a teacher spotted me opening my shirt at a girl and causing all kinds of embarrassment.

Me walking toddler Rohanna in the snow in this shirt, 2002.

2022-23 Nike blue third kit

Yes, I know Newcastle thrashed us 6-1 while wearing it but with its psychedelic design this trippy blue, turquoise number was an incredible addition to the wardrobe of many a Spurs fan.

Yet, this is probably the first choice I have made in this list people might not like and I could be fairly confident that people probably won't like it as much as some of my other choices.

But I like it and felt like we should have worn it more often.

Far superior in design than our deep-sea diver-like away kit.

Plus, we wore it when we won in Marseille so it wasn't all that bad.

2017-18 Nike home kit

Again, I'm a fan of the simple yet effective home shirts.

Sure, make the away kits zany and mad but please, whoever designs our shirts, don't desecrate the lilywhite.

Nike's first attempt at a home kit for the season we moved away from White Hart Lane and took up residency in Wembley was a corker.

With just a hint of navy blue on the slight v-neck and under the arms, it's a modest yet striking kit and is the one we played in when we beat Real Madrid at the home of football and finally shook off the Stamford Bridge hoodoo.

Memories of Dele Alli wheeling away, cupping his hand in his ear in front of home support only added to its beauty.

Kudos to the reverse away kit too.

2018-19 Nike green away kit

This one was a grower on me. When we wore it for our opening fixture up at St James' Park, I wasn't convinced. Spurs playing in green? Call me a traditionalist but the only time I want to see green on a football kit is if it's the goalkeeper's jersey, or if it's remnants of hallowed turf staining a shirt after a full-blooded slide tackle.

However, I only need to type three words and you'll forgive me for being fickle and doing a full 360-degree turn on my take for this classic. Lucas Moura. Ajax.

Thanks to our tricky Brazilian winger, this potential dud became an icon and straight after you couldn't find this strip for love or money. It's taken me nearly five years to hunt a couple down for me and my son!

Yes, the strange green design with N17 printed in its pattern was also the kit we wore when a Harry Kane-less Tottenham beat Manchester City in the quarter-finals of that season's Champions League too and now it's cemented as a classic. Just watch the club re-

release it in the next couple of decades as a retro favourite.

Honourable mention – 2000-01 Adidas blue away kit

They say that you never forget your first and I certainly don't. Christmas Day, 2000. I'm sitting with my two sisters making our way through our presents and I come across this, my first-ever Spurs shirt. It was love at first sight. Mum and Dad said that they bought it instead of the home one because they thought the darker navy blue wouldn't show as many stains (I used to play in goal before the other boys got bigger than me and kept lobbing shots from long distance) and so began my love affair with this kit and away shirts in general.

Although it doesn't quite make the top eleven, I couldn't not mention it. Yes, we lost to Derby, Leeds, Coventry, and Southampton and only ever won one game wearing it (our final home game of the 1999-2000 season in a 3-1 victory over Sunderland) but it was such a step up on the horrendous yellow and navy kit from the year before.

I didn't wear it for long. By the following winter, my growth spurts had confined it to the charity shop bag and I've been looking for a decently priced medium size ever since. Even now I purr, Waynes World style, at some of the overpriced offerings on eBay.

It will be mine, oh yes, it will be mine...again.

Mum, baby Rohanna and an 11-year-old-me, probably pulling that face because we've just lost away to Derby County in my first shirt. 2001

5

BEST MATCHES

These are the games about glory, when we won in style and with a flourish, to paraphrase Danny Blanchflower. These are the moments when our beloved Spurs took on the best in the world and won, when we won silverware (yes, really) and were really on our day. So many great moments missed the list (Dortmund, 9-1 against Wigan, victories over Man Utd at Old Trafford, our first game at the new stadium in 2019) but these moments are those that made me proud to be a lilywhite.

And yet, watching these moments back was slightly painful. Some because I miss the players that we had back then, others because I miss the people I was with when they happened and also because they really could have led us on to greater things. But in one shining glorious second in time, these moments are the ones that made me roar, cry, feel sick and throw myself on the floor in relief and exhaustion. Sometimes all at the same time!

Lucas Moura's hat-trick – Ajax 2-3 Tottenham, Champions League semi-final second leg, 2019

We all know where we were when Lucas Moura's third goal sent us into the Champions League final for the very first time in our history. We all remember how we felt and who we were with. Yet a night with so much elation and happiness had started so badly. We were missing Harry Kane, injured in the previous round, and we had been roundly beaten by the Dutch champions in the home leg at the Tottenham Hotspur Stadium. This was a team with emerging names like De Ligt, De Jong and Van Der Beek and they had dumped Juventus and Real Madrid out in previous rounds. Also, the previous night had witnessed one of the best comebacks ever with Liverpool recovering from a 3-0 defeat to Barcelona in the first match winning 4-0 at home to book their place in the final for a second consecutive year.

And so, with my West Ham mate Jamie perched on the sofa beside me, I had a bad feeling about this. Our form in the league had tanked and a side that looked like challenging for the title at Christmas was now praying it could consolidate fourth. And when De Ligt headed Ajax into the lead I just felt like the turnaround was impossible. My thoughts were confirmed minutes later when Ziyech scored past Lloris and at half-time we needed three goals in 45 minutes of football to reach the promised land. The Ajax fans felt so confident they had done it, that Bob Marley's The Little Birds started playing around the ground, really rubbing salt into the wound. It wouldn't happen, I kept telling Jamie and myself. It just doesn't happen for Tottenham. Ever.

But...every so often, a miracle occurs.

First Lucas broke after fine work from Dele Alli to slot past Onana. "Typical Spurs," I said, "Daring to raise my hopes again." Then after a goalmouth scramble in which Llorente should have scored, Lucas' feet were suddenly possessed by the spirit of Maradona and he danced past defenders to bury the ball in the onion bag again. I properly celebrated that one and yes, I did allow myself to dream again.

As time ticked away, we pushed and pushed but that all-important third goal just wasn't coming. How cruel it was when in the 87th minute Jan Vertonghen, back at the club where he started his career, headed onto the bar when he was free and then had his follow-up chance blocked on the line. I knew that was it, it wasn't to be. So near, but yet again, so far.

But wait. In the last minute of added-on time, Sissoko pumps it up the pitch to Llorente, who cushions it down for Dele Alli, who plays the deftest of lay off to Lucas Moura. He has to hit it the first time. It has to be inch-perfect as De Ligt's boot is mere millimetres away from the ball as he hits it. It flies into the bottom corner.

Pandemonium. I jump on Jamie, screaming in a high-pitched wail of disbelief. As Lucas disappears under a pile of Tottenham players we're all crying, aren't we? Poch certainly was. I had tears pouring down my cheeks.

We'd done it, the most un-Tottenham thing ever.
We'd reached the promised land.

Me at the end of the Ajax second leg, checking my heart rate. 2019

Peter Crouch's header gets us Champions League – Manchester City 0-1 Tottenham, Premier League, 2010

We've done it many times since, but in May 2010 Spurs were on the cusp of doing something they had never done in the Premier League era. Qualified for Champions League football. We'd been close, of course, in 2006 and four years on we had another young side hungry for success. But to do it, they would have to travel to play their nearest rivals for the coveted fourth-place position. Away from home, away from a stadium of fans roaring them on. They would have to beat Roberto Mancini's Manchester City – the club recently bankrolled by a Saudi state – in their backyard to make certain with a game to go that we could get there.

I couldn't focus in the day building up to the game. Work was a blur and getting back home again afterwards just made me all the more nervous as I knew time was fast approaching. My Dad couldn't join me in the village pub, he thought if he watched he'd jinx us. I nervously checked social media for any rumours of dodgy lasagne possibly thwarting us again and thankfully there were none. Most of my mates were in exam season at uni so it was just me making the trip to the pub, where thankfully many Spurs fans were congregating all buzzing with anticipation and bricking it with nerves.

I had faith. I'd seen us beat the scum and Chelsea in four days and it had given me a renewed sense of belief. I knew we could do it.

As soon as the game began, those nerves multiplied but soon I settled into the game as I saw Gareth Bale go close, Peter Crouch smack a header against the post and Jermain Defoe drew a magnificent save from former Spur Marton Fulop. As the game wore on it was no doubt Tottenham's game to win as City looked like rabbits in the headlights. Finally, in the 82nd minute, Younes Kaboul, our unlikely right-back for the game, pushed his way past Craig

Bellamy and centred a deflected cross which was palmed by Fulop into the air.

Crouchy just has to get there and nod us into ecstasy. The away end exploded, the pub exploded and drinks went everywhere. It was a goal from a player who grew up a Spurs fan who delivered us Champions League football for the very first time. Queue scenes of wild celebrations. Harry Redknapp being drowned by some of our fringe players in celebration, spending half the night up watching the goal on loop on Sky Sports News and biking 15 miles the next day to meet my girlfriend in a pub for lunch, carrying all the papers I could in my overnight bag to read and let it sink in.

Taxi for Maicon - Gareth Bale destroys Inter Milan – Tottenham 3-1 Inter Milan, 2010

When Spurs got past Young Boys in the qualifying round and were drawn with reigning champions, we were all licking our lips with the prospect of the best European side at the time coming to the Lane. But in the first encounter at the San Siro, we were outclassed. 4-0 down, Gomes sent off so we only had ten men too and we all thought it was going to be a cricket score come full-time.

Enter Gareth Bale and the match that changed his life. His devastating second-half hat trick made this the game that exposed him on the world stage and gave us our greatest-ever defeat if you catch my drift. When it came to the home tie, White Hart Lane was louder than it had ever been, there was buzz in the atmosphere and we had nothing to fear.

New signing Rafa Van der Vaart put us in the lead with a superb through ball from Luka Modrić which sliced through the Inter defence like hot butter. Then Bale began to terrorise Maicon, the Brazilian right-back whose career was never the same again after this. His first run at the Brazilian got everyone up off their seats and Peter Crouch should have done better, skewering his volley wide.

Then in the second half, Bale ran Maicon ragged time and time again and finally, Crouch got on the end of his low cross, sending White Hart Lane delirious. For the second time that night, I jumped on my Dad and he tried to swing me around in joy. Then it all got a bit nervy with ten minutes to go as Samuel E'to got one back but nothing was going to stop Bale from having the last word, breaking on the counterattack again with such power and pace no one was stopping him. He broke down the left, the clap of seats swinging up echoed around the place and once more Bale laid the ball on a plate, this time for Roman Pavlyuchenko, who just couldn't miss. A star was truly born in Bale and for us, our men in all white had delivered a Glory, Glory Night never to forget.

Kaboul's late winner completes comeback at the Emirates – A*****l 2-3 Tottenham, 2010

We never won at the Emirates. We didn't even win at Highbury when I was growing up. So, imagine my shock, horror and utter elation when it finally did happen. If you were to register your first win at your rivals' gaff in years, then surely coming back from two goals down to deny them the chance to go top of the table and ruining every single Gooner's weekend is the best way to do it?

Our league form had been a little patchy since the start of the season despite our heroics in our first Champions League campaign winning five of our first 13 league games. When Samir Nasri danced past Gomes and Benoit Assou-Ekotto to score from a tight angle, the game was only a couple of minutes old. My Dad and I both had the same sinking feeling. 'Here we go again...'

Our mood didn't improve when Marouane Chamakh doubled the Scum's lead after 27 minutes. I switched off. I went upstairs and did something different. I think I played some GTA on my Xbox and put Metallica on as I was in an angry mood and didn't want to be disturbed. Then my Dad knocked on the door to tell me that Gareth Bale had pulled on back. "Big deal," replied the moody me. I went back to my gaming and then roughly twenty minutes later my Dad burst into my room, no knock this time, and bellowed, "PENALTY...TO US!!!" No time to leap downstairs, I switched my radio on just at the right moment as Rafa Van der Vaart equalised and became an instant cult hero for raising a finger to his lips to silence the new Lighbury.

I stayed glued to that radio for the rest of the game and when Younes Kaboul rose highest to a Rafa free-kick, glancing the most perfect header into the back of the net, I screamed the house down in delight.

Then I remembered there were four minutes to go, plus stoppage time. Why does time go slower when you want it to speed up? Even listening to the radio was torture. Every Gooner attack sounded like it was going to result in a goal. I probably got my first grey hair that day. In the end, the whistle blew and my weekend was perfect. A friend's Mum was so jubilant that she wanted to plant a Spurs flag in a Gooner's garden in our village. The club was changing and I was bloody loving it.

Llorente's hip at the Etihad – Manchester City 3-4 Tottenham, Champions League quarter-final second leg, 2019

Within eleven minutes of the second leg against English rivals Manchester City, I stared aghast at what I was watching. It was 2-2, there had been four shots on target and all of them had gone in. The game, no, the world, had gone mad. We'd taken a slender 1-0 lead up to the Etihad Stadium and Pep Guardiola's City were set up to rip us to shreds. League form had become indifferent and in the face of a billion-pound winning machine, I sat on the sofa, Hummel home shirt 1985-87 on, crossing all my fingers and toes that somehow, lady luck would be smiling down upon us.

But after the opening exchanges, I genuinely had to check my reflection in the mirror to see that I hadn't gone bald from stress. One minute Sterling had curled a delicious finish past Hugo Lloris, the next Sonny capitalised on poor defending from Laporte.

Then Luca Moura wins the ball in midfield, and lays it onto Sonny who curls a brilliant strike past the despairing Ederson and suddenly we're in dreamland!

Then Bernardo Silva goes and ruins it by slapping one in off Danny Rose's arse before Sterling pierces our defence again after 21 minutes. By half-time, I felt like I needed gas and air. My heart couldn't cope. The Fitbit on my wrist must have thought I was on a run! Knowing that we'd had supremacy now it all hinged on who scored first in the second half and the tension was harrowing. When Sergio Aguero buried a hard shot into the net with half an hour to go, I knew the inevitable was about to happen. We'd crash out, the memes would be unbearable and I'd have to find my thick skin to take all the "banter".

But then, a corner from Kieran Trippier found the hip of Fernando Llorente and the ball sailed past Ederson and suddenly, we were through on away goals. I nearly punched a hole in the ceiling I celebrated so hard. So imagine my horror when it went to VAR for handball. Thankfully, the angle the referee saw looked like our Spanish striker hadn't handled the ball and it was given. Then I thought, "shit, we've got seventeen minutes left of the game!"

Queue my fingernails being chewed to the cuticles. When Eriksen played a stupid backpass to Aguero, leading to a heartbreaking goal from Sterling, the Etihad erupted, Pep was taking his cardigan off and running around like a man on fire and I had fully inserted my fist into my other hand, cursing our luck and moaning, "why does it always happen to us?"

But wait, there's a check on the goal. Turns out Eriksen had played the ball onto a City player and Aguero was offside when it fell to him. The goal was disallowed. The Eithad fell quiet, except for us Spurs fans. I ran back into the living room and fell to my knees just as Pep did the same on the touchline.

The full-time whistle blows, we're in the Champions League semi-final and despite being exhausted from watching such an incredible game, sleep is the last thing that I want to do that night. What a game.

Harry Kane breaks Jimmy Greaves' record – Tottenham 1-0 Manchester City, Premier League, 2023

Me with the great Jimmy Greaves, now our second highest scorer, 2013

I could have gone for his first North London derby when he announced himself to White Hart Lane as the new hero. I could also have gone for the 5-3 win over Chelsea in which he began to dominate the Premier League but in the end, it had to be this one for me. Growing up I was always told about the great Jimmy Greaves and his 266 goals for Tottenham and how that would never be eclipsed. Then along came Harry Kane. A goal machine, a player with such finishing technique the great Greaves gave him full approval early in his career. Then, on that night in N17, as he latched onto a Pierre-Emile Højbjerg pass and slotted past the stranded Ederson, history was made.

Harry Kane was now Tottenham Hotspur's all-time top goal scorer. A decades-old record had fallen at the feet of one of our own. And then...well, to tell you the truth, I missed the rest of the game. I had a gig booked that night so kept tabs on the match as we travelled to it. I felt too nervous to check my phone when it buzzed after putting it away, just in case Pep Guardiola's all-conquering Champions had found a way back into the game. But they never did. We even gave them a nudge to do so when Cristian Romero sent Jack Grealish tumbling and saw red.

But City's comically bad record at the Tottenham Hotspur Stadium was built upon as Harry's solitary goal was enough to see him at the top of our charts and our hearts and become an immortal.

When I watched it all back when I got home, I loved seeing how overjoyed his teammates were for him. For the "hasn't won any trophies" brigade, it takes luck, let alone just being in a gifted squad in which you're not a first-teamer, to say that you are a winner. Just ask Scott Carson.

But it takes skill, determination, guts and loyalty to do what Harry did.

And for that, to be around to witness Tottenham's greatest make history, it makes my list.

Dele Alli destroys the best team in the World – Tottenham 3-1 Real Madrid, Champions League, 2017

My view as Tottenham were about to take on Real Madrid, 2017

Remember our season and a half at the home of English football? How can many of us forget? Having to travel to the other side of London was a difficult proposition for me but I had done it for the Champions League games the previous season. Then, when we were drawn into a group with the holders and the most famous team in the world Real Madrid, I just had to get back to Wembley. I parked up at

Stanmore, made the short journey in and pinched myself at how lucky I was.

I evoked the pre-match ritual I had going the previous season. I booked myself a table at Gurkha Valley curry house just near the pub so I could properly set myself up before meeting my friend Nick, who had got me a ticket because his sister was now unable to attend. I felt so grateful to be there, regardless of the score at the end of the game. It was a pinch-yourself moment and as the teams came out, I thought about my Dad and how I wished he was there too.

It's a night I will never forget. The night that Tottenham Hotspur, resplendent in their all-white kit, tore the European champions a new one. We were sensational from start to finish. Deservedly went in front through a poke home from Dele Alli. Harry Winks, who was superb on the night, played a cross-field ball to Kieran Trippier. The right-back was offside, but what did we care? VAR wasn't around and we were beating Real Madrid!

After the break, having soaked up a lot of pressure from the likes of Ronaldo, Kroos, Modrić and Benzema, we doubled our lead! I could have jumped out of the stadium at that point I was so elated. Alli smashed the ball against Sergio Ramos – who Mousa Dembele owned later in the game – and the deflection took us two goals up. And it got better.

Alli again was central to proceedings as he fed Harry Kane, who in a reversal of roles fed the ball on a plate to Christian Eriksen to tap home. I was in line with Kane, begging him to pass to the great Dane, who had acres of space around him. The roof came off Wembley that night. That settled it. We were about to beat the Galacticos. Even Ronaldo's late consolation, the crush on the train to the station and the roadworks that meant I didn't get home until one in the morning on a work day couldn't take the smile off my face.

Thrashing the Arse 5-1 – Tottenham 5-1 A*****l, Carling Cup semi-final second leg, 2008

Of all the games I wish I had gone to, this was it. The first time we had crushed the scum in nine years and I was in my local pub, as usual around this time, sinking as many Jack Daniels and cokes as I could to settle the nerves. We'd looked so good in the first leg yet given a late equaliser away and in the previous year this exact fixture had played out as a defeat but something felt different this time. Ledley played at the back and the team just looked up for it.

Any early nerves began to dissipate when Jermaine Jenas put us one nil up on two minutes. Twenty minutes or so later, a Bentner own goal had almost gotten rid of them completely but this was Tottenham we were talking about and the year before we had been two-nil to the good and thrown it away. Not this time though.

After half-time, Robbie Keane half-volleyed a beauty past Flabby-handski who helped it into the bottom corner of the net. 3-0. We were thrashing them. Me and my mates couldn't believe it. Yet one of them was still on the edge of his seat, biting his nails. However, as we were 4-1 up on aggregate, every five minutes that ticked by, he relaxed a little. I kept saying to him that the Gooners weren't coming back from this, especially after Aaron Lennon made it four, but when Emmanuel Adebayor pulled one back, he shot me a look like it was all my fault.

Luckily, it was my round next and I got them in as the crowd at White Hart Lane roared with such ferocious energy I had never heard before. We were going to Wembley, no matter what happened now and Steed Malbranque's late strike meant that we had repeated the 5-1 scoreline over Chelsea in 2002 and now we were there. Back in a cup final and after such an emphatic scoreline, I truly felt the League Cup was ours. I went home singing and dancing, my Dad was already watching the highlights and taping them for prosperity. I called my Grandad the next morning and told him I had seen the greatest game in my lifetime. Then he reminded me, "It means nothing if we don't win the final." I didn't share that sentiment but it did remind me of who we had waiting for us there...

Ledley lifts the League Cup – Chelsea 1-2 Tottenham – Carling Cup final, 2008

The Chelsea team of the time was truly formidable. Twice Premier League champions, owner Roman Abramovich had bankrolled a squad of world-class talent built around two English players John Terry and Frank Lampard. They were all-conquering it felt and on the morning of the game, as I text my pals to see who was venturing to the local pub to watch it, I felt more excitement than dread in facing such a side.

We weren't doing very well at the time. Juande Ramos had come in and steadied the ship but I had seen Robbie Keane and Dimitar Berbatov striking up a partnership so deadly that anybody would struggle to play against them. Ledley King had also been rested and our two new defensive recruits Jonathan Woodgate and Alan Hutton had made us look more stable at the back in recent games.

One by one I rounded my Spurs mates up and off we trudged to the local. It was pretty much standing room only as the giant projector screen greeted us. One side of the pub was full of Lilywhite shirts, the other royal blue as division lines were drawn. Then the game kicked off and we were straight out of the traps. Keano nearly broke the deadlock in under a minute and Pascal Chimbonda – who was playing at left-back due to injuries to Gareth Bale and Lee-Young Pyo, hit the crossbar with a looping header.

Then Chelsea scored. Of course they did. One-half of the place melted into a sea of sighs, the other with wild jubilation. The songs were being sung louder by the Chelsea lot and yet I still kept the faith. It was unfair we'd gone behind having played the better football but so much of the game was left.

Then, when Wayne Bridge juggled the ball with his hand, I shot up along with my comrades appealing for a penalty. It was given and when I saw Berba step up to take it, I knew this was a goal already. 1-1. Then Didier Zokora went through on goal and somehow missed. He clobbered his strike into Petr

Cech's face then blasted the rebound over the bar whilst our favourite Bulgarian striker implored him to pass. At that point, I remembered the pain I felt when Blackburn beat us six years previously and all of a sudden I started to feel like it wasn't our day.
Jonathan Woodgate would prove me wrong and his scrappy header at the start of extra time put us two goals up. Then came nearly half an hour of torment as wave upon wave of Chelsea attacks pummeled our goal but Paul Robinson was equal to them and as the Tottenham flags were waving all around and the full-time whistle blew during another Chelsea attack, it sealed glory. We all celebrated and my family came down to partake in the knees up. I made a drunken phone call to my Grandad and the rest of the day is lost to the mists of time. We'd done it. We'd beaten two of our biggest rivals and as Ledley and Keano lifted the trophy I'd seen us win something after nine long years in the wilderness. Glory, glory hallelujah!!

Kane and Son ruin A*****l's season – Tottenham 3-0 A*****l, Premier League, 2022

At a time when Mikel Arteta had looked to steady the sinking Gooner ship, we had also turned around our patchy form at the start of the campaign and now both teams were battling it out for the coveted fourth place. A fixture which had been pushed back from December, after the Scum had pleaded with the FA to move it following a case of COVID in their camp, making such a joke of guidelines it made them look like cowards. For us, we were still four points behind them, having played a game more and defeat would gift our most hated rivals Champions League football next year. Truth be told though, we weren't worried. As I settled down to watch the game and allowed the atmosphere from a balmy Tottenham Hotspur Stadium to echo around my living room, it reminded me of our 5-1 victory years earlier. The crowd just seemed to have a feeling.

That feeling was transmitted onto the pitch as Harry Kane, the top scorer in these derbies, slotted home another penalty against that lot in the 22nd minute. Then he later stooped low to head in unmarked from a Rodrigo Bentancur flick-on. The place erupted, and I jumped up and down. No way were we going to let the first NLD with fans inside our home ground slip away from us. In between, their defender Rob Holding was done twice by Sonny, the second challenge resulting in a red card, meaning that the Gooners would have to face us for nearly an hour with ten men.

We looked hungry and ready to kill the game and just after half-time, Sonny pounced to make it three. At that point, I thought we would get more but we seemed to just toy with them, like a cat with a mouse. Arteta's face was a picture near the end and at the final whistle, we'd not only beaten the Scum but beaten them well.

Even if they'd had eleven men on the pitch, they weren't escaping without a punishment from our boys and now they were truly looking over their shoulders. Three days later they went to St James

Park and lost 2-0 to Newcastle. It all but confirmed their humiliation and our glory as we pipped them to the post. The fact it was against them made it so, so sweet. It shut up some Goons I have known for a while, too.

Farewell to the Lane – Tottenham 2-1 Manchester United, Premier League, 2017

I last visited the old place during its penultimate season in a 3-0 win against Bournemouth but considering my Father had passed away less than a year previously it proved to be a painful experience going back knowing he wasn't there, or that I wouldn't be calling him up any time during the day to let him know how we'd played. When it was confirmed that the 2016-17 season would be our last at the iconic White Hart Lane, I couldn't bring myself to go. As my self-imposed exile wore on that year, I saw more and more of that lovely old place disappear. First, the corner of the Paxton Road end was demolished and then, like a vast shadow the new stadium began to engulf the old.

Every home game that year felt like it was the last of something. We'd won the final North London derby, finished above the Scum for the first time since I became a fan and now, in the last-ever match, we could finish the season unbeaten on our home turf. My then-girlfriend (now my wife) had booked for us to go to dinner that day around kick-off time, in a pub which had TVs built into the booths. I was looking forward to it but also hoping I didn't become a blubbering wreck at the full-time whistle.

Victor Wanyama got us off to the best possible start, sending a bullet header past David de Gea to give the White Hart Lane faithful something to add to the occasion. Then just after half-time, Harry Kane scored first ever goal against Man Utd and subsequently the final Spurs goal at the Lane. Wayne Rooney poked home and ruined the poetic notion that one of our own would get the final goal at the old place but as the final whistle blew, and the fans poured onto the pitch, I did wish that I was there to drink it all in too. Sure, as a member I'd be getting a key chain with a piece of the turf inside it to remember the place by, but I felt a real pang of missing out.

Then when the crowd went back to their seats, we moved to the main bar in the pub. Although Sophie was getting bored by the whole thing, the occasion felt special to me. Seeing those old clips, then as the heavens opened heroes from the past marched onto the pitch, followed by our current squad and then that mixture of history and the now seemed to marry so well together given the fact the the old and new stadium stood side-by-side too.

Then matchday interviewer Paul Coyte reminded us that generations of families had come to the Lane and I welled up. I remembered my first trip with my Dad and pictured what it must have been like for my Grandad and Great-Grandad when they were there too. When the bloke from the Go Compare ads started singing Glory, Glory Hallelujah, I wasn't the only one in the pub with leaky eyes.

Then, at the crescendo, a rainbow formed over White Hart Lane. It was almost as though it was a gift from those who couldn't be there to let us know that the spirit of so many people would stay with that old ground. That rainbow and the pitch invasion at the end will live with me forever. Yes, it was old, and yes it wasn't as big or state-of-the-art as the Tottenham Hotspur Stadium we know and love now but White Hart Lane was a cathedral, a place families went to together and shared across generations in one mutual love.

Mine and Sophie's booth before kick-off, where I saw the Lane Finale, 2017

White Hart Lane always felt so special. The matchday rituals, the getting off the train at Northumberland Park, past the chippy and the Spurs shop on the corner, looking out for the cockerel standing proudly in the skyline. That feeling of togetherness with strangers, knowing that you were all friends here. The matchday programme stalls, the burger and hot dog stands, the merchandise stalls, the coppers on their horses and clapping the team bus as it made its way down Bill Nicholson Way. Then, you'd start to hear sounds coming from inside the ground and even as an adult, I'd implore my Dad to let us go find our seats. The clicking of the turnstiles, the blank concrete nothingness inside the ground and then walking up the steps to be greeted by the green pitch and the incredible sight of the stadium in front of you. I miss it so much, that old place and I miss the people I used to go with.

White Hart Lane will always, and forever be my second home.

In the directors box on the tour of White Hart Lane, 2006

HALF TIME

RIVALRIES AND THE MANAGERS

6

RIVALRIES

Every hero needs a villain. A Joker to their Batman. A Playstation to their Nintendo and the beauty of such rivalries is that no matter how much you hate them, there will always be a time when you will come out on top. Here is a rogue's gallery of teams I simply cannot stand. Some are self-explanatory, others less so but still, I'm sure that after I've explained my case, you'll love to hate them too.

A*****l
Best win in the Premier League era: Tottenham 2-0 Arsenal, last derby at White Hart Lane, 2017.
Worst defeat in the Premier League era: Arsenal 3-0 Tottenham, Highbury, 2002.

We all know the stories. The fact that they moved from South London onto our patch, bribed their way into the league and got us relegated in the process, became a franchise under Herbert Chapman, won the league at our ground twice, stole our club captain and adopted a hateful celebration in St Totteringhams Day for every season they mathematically finish ahead of us. All of that aside, my hatred for that other lot also got personal, considering that during their invincible season, my best friend was a Gooner, so the jibes were especially pointed at a time when we were managerless and falling down the table.

And there were all the years where it looked like we would overtake them as top dogs in London. We'd beat them at the Lane as Arsey Winger's charges seemed to be running out of steam. Indeed, with a few games to go, AVB even once remarked that they were in a "downward spiral" as we soared to third seemingly on course for supremacy. And yet, they always managed to claw it back.

I was so dejected after we finished the 2012-13 season a point behind them, despite our record points tally in the Premier League era, that I had an argument with my Spurs friend who I'd invited over to watch the game and stormed off that evening to the pub in a grump and nearly had a fight. I thought that we'd never finish above them.

Thank God it all changed and we got to enjoy several years of us finishing above them. All those Harry Kane goals, the wins at WHL, Wembley and the Tottenham Hotspur Stadium. I even descend into fits of laughter when they lose, especially when they have lost in a humiliating fashion and gone all "Arsey". I mean, imagine being so far ahead in the Premier League title race and still losing to Manchester City. When the Goons eff up, it's like Christmas. And thankfully, even though we still have no trophies to shout about, that lot from South London can always be relied on to be the gift that keeps on giving.

Chelsea

Best win in the Premier League era: Chelsea 1-3 Tottenham, Stamford Bridge, 2018.
Worst defeat in the Premier League era: Tottenham 1-6 Chelsea, White Hart Lane, 1997.

There are days in the week when I truly hate Chelsea more than our North London counterparts and the hatred runs back many a decade for older fans. My Father used to say that, until the 1967 FA Cup Final – the first all-London final – Chelsea had always just been an annoyance more than a fierce rival. Then when we relegated them in the mid-seventies, aggravating an already aggressive hooligan fanbase against our firm, it spilled into all-out war.

To say that the scales have tipped against them in the time since then would be an understatement and I grew up in a world where Spurs would be beaten every single season by their blue rivals. It wasn't helped that nineties Chelsea, with the metropolitan big names and celebrity fans, seemed the more attractive club to follow for many of my friends and this was further cemented when a certain Russian billionaire was supposed to be taking a look at our gaff but flew over West London instead, bought them out and revolutionised them into an all-conquering side.

Even when they seem to be having a laughably bad season, they will always get the better of us and although the scales have tipped marginally in our favour in the last ten years, we still can't seem to buy a win over them at Stamford Bridge. Just one win there in 34 years is truly astonishing but no matter what the state of their club is, there is nothing that they love more than to ruin our campaign, and frustratingly, they have done that very, very often.

Which makes the odd time we have eclipsed them taste all that much sweeter. The Carling Cup final in 2008, Modrić's winner at the Lane the year after, Bale dismantling them in 2010, Kane coming to the fore in the incredible 5-3 victory, the Dele Alli double at their gaff and the 3-1 win in our times at Wembley were particularly satisfying but now that Poch is managing them, and that they ruined our season early in the 2023-24 campaign, I hate them all the more.

I can't wait until FFP catches up with them...

West Ham
Best win in the Premier League era: Tottenham 4-0 West Ham, White Hart Lane, 2015
Worst defeat in the Premier League era: Tottenham 1-4 West Ham, White Hart Lane, 1994

A bit of a one-sided rivalry in this one. The Hammers, my mate Jamie aside, simply cannot stand us. For decades we've eclipsed them, nicked their better players off them, had run-ins in which we've come out on top, scored late winners, almost relegated them, and ruined their "cup final" almost annually and yet for some reason, they still don't like us...

Not that there is much love lost going the other way and in truth, I don't mind them. For a club who have given us such gems in the Premier League years as Jermaine Defoe, Michael Carrick, Freddie Kanoute and Scott Parker we've gifted them Matt Etherington, Bobby Zamora, Sergei Rebrov, Robbie Keane and Les Ferdinand, all when they have been surplus to requirements. I can't hate them. However, they seem to detest us back.

Is it because of Paul Stalteri's late winner to leave them on the brink of relegation in 2007? Or Gareth Bale's incredible last-minute winner on the 20th anniversary of Bobby Moore's passing in 2013? Or Eric Dier's debut last-minute winner over them in 2015? Or Harry Kane's late double in added time to snatch victory from the jaws of defeat in 2017? Or the fact that at one point we'd won more games at the London Stadium against them than they had beaten us there? Or that we laughed when their beloved Upton Park was blown up for a film?

Possibly.

Perhaps all this history carries the real reason why I hate one aspect of West Ham and it's the fans. Jamie and former podcasting pal Mark aside, who are real gems, every other West Ham fan I know goes well overboard when they beat us. When they were the first side to beat Spurs at the Tottenham Hotspur Stadium, the memes and social media messages were ridiculous. You'd have thought they'd won the league. When lasagnegate happened, they celebrated like they'd got Champions League qualification that day. The hundreds of fans who gathered outside the London Stadium with flares (the guns, not the trousers) to celebrate Spurs losing the Champions League final, they can get to feck. Those who wore t-shirts proudly reminding us that they had beaten us three times in one season. Why not hire an open-top bus while you're at it?

No wonder that in a 2018 poll, Spurs were listed as West Ham's most bitter rivals, even over Millwall (interestingly, Chelsea fans also polled us as their most hated club, bore off and go and hate Fulham!) but still, be better rivals.

Stop being pithy.

Liverpool
Best win in the Premier League era: Tottenham 4-1 Liverpool, Wembley, 2017
Worst defeat in the Premier League era: Tottenham 0-5 Liverpool, 2013

This is a pretty new rivalry I guess but I hate Liverpool for several reasons. Firstly, they destroyed my hopes and dreams by beating us in the Champions League final, putting me in a football depression that I will possibly never get out of. That game alone puts them in this category. Secondly, their fans are odd. Not all of them, of course not, but there seems to be more of a cult with regards to following Liverpool that seems to envelop some of their supporters and fill the emotional void where something else is lacking. Maybe it's Bill Shankly's fault with that ridiculous, "football is more important than life and death" rhetoric? Possibly, but the fans in my life who take to social media and cry about conspiracy theories and fixture congestion that other clubs who are successful also has to deal with, honestly, it's nauseating.

Which brings me to my third point. Jürgen Klopp. I can't stand him. His over-the-top fist punches every time they win a game. The way his nice guy act drops whenever they have a whiffy result. His conduct against journalists and when he stokes the fire within those keyboard warriors and almost encourages them with his complaints. Look at how he acted after we beat them 2-1 in a game when VAR let Liverpool down. He said there should be a replay. Christ! He said it would be fair if we replayed the game. Why? For nearly every game we've played them since 2019, VAR has robbed us of a decision or two that may have seen us come out on top against Liverpool.

There's Sissoko's handball in the Champions League final. Skipp got kicked in the head by Diogo Jota, who didn't get a red card despite the dangerous play. VAR ruling out Spurs goals for being offside by a centimetre, christ, let's replay all of them, shall we Jürgen?

And that's my fourth point. The infamous 2023 League clash aside, we've had no good luck against that lot. Some fans think this might be down to Klopp's constant moaning which has led to influencing the referee's decisions in games against us. And their fans went way overboard when Harry Kane was up against Mo Salah for a golden boot and our Harry claimed a goal against Stoke when it looked like he didn't touch it.

Still, when we do beat them victory tastes very sweet, but I'd give it all away and swap it for that Champions League game to go our way.

Leicester City
Best win in the Premier League era: Leicester 1-6 Tottenham, King Power Stadium, 2017
Worst defeat in the Premier League era: Leicester 4-1 Tottenham, King Power Stadium, 2023

Recent history aside, it's fair to say that Spurs have had a bit of a stranglehold on the Foxes. From beating them in the 1961 FA Cup final to completing the double to Allan Nielsen's last-minute winner against them in the League Cup in 1999, we've thwarted them on more than one occasion. No wonder they really cannot stand us.

The title challenge in 2016 was manufactured by the media (we were never top, always playing catch-up whilst the league seemed to be lying down to let this "miracle" of Leicester winning the title) but we will never forget those jubilant scenes in Jamie Vardy's kitchen when Eden Hazard equalised against us and since then our encounters have been tastier.

Overall, we've had more standout moments against them, with Harry Kane and Heung-Min Son helping themselves to hattricks against them in 2017 and 2022 respectively, but ever since that 2016 run-in, I've wanted nothing more than for us to end their season whenever we play. It was hilarious when Gareth Bale scored two late goals to stop them from getting Champions League football on the final day of the season in 2021 and I laughed my head off when we thrash them now and again.

Sure, they can sing about the Premier League and the FA Cup but...ah, eff off back to the Midlands.

Plus, I find Jamie Vardy an ignorant prick.

Newcastle United
Best win in the Premier League era: Tottenham 5-0 Newcastle, White Hart Lane, 2012
Worst defeat in the Premier League era: Newcastle 7-1 Tottenham, St James' Park, 1996

Another club who seems to hate us more than we hate them. My memories of our games against the Toon Army are of one thing - goals, and plenty of them. Over the years there haven't been too many dull 0-0 draws between us and for a long time we seemed to get one over on them up on Tyneside then they'd come to N17 and return the favour!

For every 5-0 win there is an appalling 7-1 or 6-1 defeat. Even a 5-1 in which we crumbled up at St James' Park and an already relegated Newcastle stopped us from finishing above Arsenal for the first time in what felt like a millennium. There was Nikos Dabizas' handball that wasn't given in the FA Cup semi-final in 1999 and those appalling defeats at home in 2013, 2014 and 2015. But what have they got against Spurs? Nothing, as far as I can tell. Even now I think they just do it to annoy us.

They are now Saudi-owned, possibly the last state-owned Premier League side for quite some time and that adds even more needle now that we will be hoping to challenge them at the top of the table.

It's always a good night when we do them and I hope we continue to slap them up in future, if for nothing else but to wipe that silly grin off Jacob Murphy's mouth.

Charlton Athletic
Best win in the Premier League era: Tottenham 5-1 Charlton, White Hart Lane, 2006
Worst defeat in the Premier League era: Charlton 3-1 Tottenham, Valley Parade, 2001

Another side whose league clashes are consigned to the history books but for a few years in the early 2000s Charlton always seemed to prove a thorn in our side. They had a pretty decent side back then too, when managed by Alan Curbishley. The likes of Scott Parker, Darren Bent, Danny Murphy (who all ended up playing for us), Dein Kiely, Shaun Bartlett and Matt Holland always gave us a good game and more often than not would beat us once a season. I used to hate it when they beat us mainly because it was so frustrating to lose to yet another London side but we also had some really good games against them.

There was the FA Cup fourth-round comeback when they went 2-0 up and we beat them 4-2 at The Valley. We repeated the same trick in the 2005-06 season after giving them a two-goal head start, this time emerging 3-2 victors. But then there were narrow 1-0 defeats in the 2001-02 and 2003-04 seasons which stung, mainly because they always seemed to do it against us when we were having a bad run and seeing the name Charlton on the fixture list always made me think we should beat them and yet, sadly, we didn't.

Our last two matches in the Prem against them were particularly memorable for me as our 5-1 win at White Hart Lane in December 2006 coincided with my first trip to London with my mates without our parents (we were all 17, it was like being on day release!) and seeing some friends Dads getting on the same train as us and chatting with them, feeling like a grown-up. I remember being in HMV on Oxford Street trying out the new Nintendo Wii when my Dad texted to say that we'd won 5-1.

And then, in one of the final games of the season, Dimitar Berbatov scored a fantastic goal against them which, coupled with a late Jermain Defoe strike, sent the Addicks down. Again, I got a text from my Dad telling me the score while I was at the pub.

So, it wasn't all bad memories against Charlton!

QPR
Best win in the Premier League era: Tottenham 4-0 QPR, White Hart Lane, 2014
Worst defeat in the Premier League era: QPR 4-1 Tottenham, Loftus Road, 1992

A rivalry in two parts as I don't recall our battles with QPR in the nineties. The Hoops had built an impressive side earlier in that decade and shared players and management alike with us in Les Ferdinand, Clive Wilson, Andy Sinton, Neil Ruddock and Gerry Francis all representing us at some point and yet, after 1996, we didn't play QPR again in the league for 15 years so all those clashes just seem to fade for me I'm afraid.

But with QPR back in the big time, we had some tasty encounters during the Harry Redknapp era, a manager who also went on to coach them. I was there to watch Gareth Bale and Rafael Van der Vaart rip them to shreds in a great 3-1 win (the same day I saw Ray Wilkins in the car park, asked him who he thought would win today, he asked me who I supported then said, "Well, you then!").

But QPR also beat us 1-0 late on that season on what would be Ledley King's final appearance for us. And we were having a stinking run of form then too, so for knackering Ledley (okay, he was already ruined but they killed him in my eyes for good) and ruining our hopes for Champions League qualification, they could get in the bin every game we met after that.

Then they went on, under overly ambitious chairman Tony Fernandes, to try and buy their way to the top and in doing so bought half our squad. There was Adel Taraabt, Jermain Jenas, Steven Caulker, Radek Cerny, Bobby Zamora, Luke Young, Andros Townsend, and Tom Carroll, thrust in with has-beens Rio Ferdinand and Rob Green. No wonder they got relegated again in 2013 and then 2015, which by that point our games against them were no contest.

Still, can't stand them for killing Ledley's career.

Wimbledon

Best win in the Premier League era: Wimbledon 2-6 Tottenham, Selhurst Park, 1998
Worst defeat in the Premier League era: Wimbledon 3-1 Tottenham, Selhurst Park, 1998

Younger readers may be crying out who? Indeed, my memories of our tussles with the Wombles of Wimbledon are a little vague now as it was such a long time ago, but there was a time when a clash with the Dons ended up with half our team being hacked off the pitch in the face of Vinnie Jones, Ben Thatcher and John Fashanu.

The Crazy Gang were a team of true brutes and did for some of our players in the past, with Mabbutt's eye socket being shattered by Fashanu's elbow in a deliberate piece of actual bodily harm. And due to their physical nature and long-ball tactics, almost all of the Premier League hated them. It was good riddance when they finally went down in 2000, with our home win that April helping to shut the lid on their time in the top flight.

I disliked them because their style of football was at odds with ours. And they were bloody nasty. Since the club folded and split into two entities (AFC Wimbledon and the MK Dons) it's pretty safe to say that those Crazy Gang days are a thing of the past now.

Manchester United
Best win in the Premier League era: Manchester United 1-6 Tottenham, Old Trafford, 2020
Worst defeat in the Premier League era: Tottenham 0-4 Man Utd, White Hart Lane, 2007

"Lads, it's Tottenham."

The only three little words that, allegedly, Sir Alex Ferguson said to his all-conquering red devils before strutting out and giving us another battering. It's the smug, overconfident and arrogant manner in which United used to speak of others, their success in England and on the continent and the longevity of it all which led to me hating Manchester United.

How different it is now. Sure, they'll finish above us or win a trophy every few years or so, but the shine has well and truly gone from the club and nowadays we fight on a more even keel than way back when. It doesn't matter whether we play at home or away, our chances of beating United have gone up massively since they were knocked off their perch, not just as the best side in England, but the best side in Manchester.

Okay, in the past two decades, they have still walloped us a few times but one of our many hoodoos of failing to win at Old Trafford is a thing of the past now.

One thing is still guaranteed though when we meet. Goals, action and ex-players on Sky Sports giving horrendously biased options on it all.

Manchester City

Best win in the Premier League era: Manchester City 0-1 Tottenham, Etihad Stadium, 2010
Worst defeat in the Premier League era: Manchester City 6-0 Tottenham, Etihad Stadium, 2013

In an astonishing twist of good fortune, the Saudi state-owned bully boys of the 2010s and onwards Manchester City seem to have an Achilles heel for us. Hilarious as it is that even when we moved into the Tottenham Hotspur Stadium, Pep Guardiola's charges have so far, at the time of writing, failed to pick up any points there in the Premier League. They haven't even registered a goal.

Back in the day when we were both battling it out for mid-table supremacy, both sides exchanged blows to one another's seasons, such as the 5-2 defeat they inflicted on us in 1994-95, but since their takeover in 2008, our fixtures against the blue side of Manchester have seen us do battle for Champions League places and even challenging for the title on a few occasions.

They hate us because we are their bogey team and we hate them because they've cheated their way to multiple trophies. As I write this, they are currently under investigation with 115 charges of Financial Fair Play breaches, so who knows? They might end up being stripped of their titles. And I might end up winning the Balon d'Or.

While we hope for that outcome, we can take solace that whoever of their big names line up against us, be it such illustrious names as Vincent Kompany, David Silva, Yaya Toure, Sergio Aguero, Phil Foden, Erling Haaland and Kevin de Bruyne, no matter where we are in the league and how bad our form is, we'll probably end up spanking them.

7

THE MANAGERS
(In the Premier League era – 1992 onwards)

Doug Livermore and Ray Clemence
Games in charge: 51 (23 wins, 11 draws, 17 defeats)
Win percentage: 45.10%
Highest Premier League finish: 8th
Most memorable moment: League double over the Scum

This is such an odd one to me as it was a couple of years before I was even aware that football was a thing. Livermore and Clemence were our first managers in the Premier League era and worked under Terry Venables, who had come down from the executive box to be more hands-on with the running of the team. Yet, the two coaches were in charge on match days. An odd experiment in management that could have brought us glory, all for a Tony Adams goal against the run of play that saw the Scum dump us out of the FA Cup at the semi-final stage.

Many of the building blocks were put in place by Livermore/Clemence as we transitioned from the Lineker/Gascoigne years to a side brimming with attacking talent, and new signing Teddy Sheringham's goals saw him win the Golden Boot and take us to 8th in the table.

The duo saw our last league double over our fiercest rivals but crunching defeats to Leeds (5-0!), Sheffield United (6-0!), Liverpool (6-2!!) and eventual winners Manchester United (4-1) served as an early warning to the issues that would plague us the following year.

All was not well upstairs and after Alan Sugar sacked Venables, Livermore and Clemence were out the door and a former favourite was needed to step in and stop the fans from lynching our trigger-happy chairman.

Osvaldo Ardiles (1993-94)
Games in charge: 56 (17 wins, 14 draws, 25 defeats)
Win percentage: 30.36%
Highest Premier League finish: 15th
Most memorable moment: The famous five

Poor Ossie Ardiles. Not only did our favourite Argentine inherit an imbalanced squad but he then decided to stack the scales so top-heavy with attacking talent that they plummeted to the floor.

The club was in permanent disarray throughout his 16 months in charge, whether that be on the pitch or off it, and Ardiles' remit was to distract the fans from the problems in the board (and court!) room and to entertain the masses. How he was supposed to do this with a back line that was so lacking and injury-ravaged was beyond him.

Thankfully, he managed to keep us up on the penultimate day of the 1993-94 season and was then the man in charge when Spurs scooped the world.

When Jürgen Klinsmann joined it gave Ardiles his chance to play a five-man attack. Unfortunately, his methods were flawed and following some ropey performances against Notts County (0-3) in the cup and heavy defeats to Man City, Leicester and Nottingham Forest in the league, he was sacked in November.

Gerry Francis (1994-97)
Games in charge: 142 (55 wins, 42 draws, 45 defeats)
Win percentage: 38.73%
Highest Premier League finish: 7th
Most memorable moment: FA Cup run in 1994-95

A frontrunner for the England job the previous year, after he had led QPR to the top six in the Premier League table, Gerry Francis looked like a safe pair of hands after a period of turmoil for Tottenham. Indeed, he shored up the defence, losing only 5 matches in the league after taking over before Christmas.

However, Francis seemed to have the rug repeatedly pulled from under his feet. In his first close summer, Spurs lost influential players like Klinsmann, Gica Popescu, Nick Barmby and almost Darren Anderton as an exodus of talent drained the squad. In their place came the likes of experienced heads Ruel Fox, Andy Sinton, Clive Wilson and even Les Ferdinand later on, sending the age of the squad upwards. Alan Sugar's transfers at this time reflect how badly burnt he felt by the likes of Klinsmann and Popescu's quick departures as our transfer targets became more conservative.

So did our football and despite Chris Armstrong blowing away all doubters in his first season, the Francis years are a period of mediocrity on the field. By the time Teddy Sheringham leapt to join Manchester United, he was leaving a club, and a manager, bereft of confidence and belief. Francis also struggled with personal issues around this time and following a bad 4-0 away defeat to Liverpool, he resigned.

For nearly a decade, Francis would arguably remain our best manager in the Premier League era and he led us on the ultimately doomed FA Cup run in 1995, after we'd been banned before Sugar got it overturned, and he managed to beat the Scum twice at home.

Christian Gross (1997-98)
Games in charge: 30 (10 wins, 8 draws, 12 defeats)
Win percentage: 33.33%
Highest Premier League finish: 14th
Most memorable moment: The infamous train ticket

You know how it is. You see the bloke you hate and the woman he's managed to pull and think, "I can get one better than him." Well, that's what Alan Sugar thought when he went continental and brought in Christian Gross in the wake of Arsène Wenger's success at the other lot's place. And whilst Wenger turned out to be their Miss World (please, don't think too hard about it, I'm already sick of myself for using this analogy), Gross lived up to his name.

In your debut home game, it's not a good sign if you lose 6-1 to Chelsea, even if the team is pretty crap. The omens were bad and Gross' new methods did little to warm the squad to him. He insisted on players staying away from their families the night before home games in a bid to gel his team together. He looked out of his depth and even though he attempts to come across as a nice guy while brandishing his tube ticket, the players saw him as anything but. Gary Mabbutt and Jürgen Klinsmann nearly led a revolt at this time and were poised to take over the team to save the club from going down!

In the end, we finished 14th and survived by the skin of our teeth and after a tepid pre-season that saw Paulo Tremanzani come through the door, Sugar had seen enough again and Gross was a goner.

Although his career continued to be a successful one in Switzerland, he never managed in England again and will forever be remembered as the man who waved his tube ticket at the press when he arrived.

George Graham (1998-2001)
Games in charge: 126 (50 wins, 35 draws, 41 defeats)
Win percentage: 39.68%
Highest Premier League finish: 10th
Most memorable moment: Worthington Cup final win, 1999

This leads us nicely to the man with the raincoat! When George Graham crossed the great divide in N17 fans were furious. I remember radio shows like 606 and my own Dad's views being particularly visceral but the enigma is, George Graham won us a trophy.

He did what so many of his successors have failed to do and led us to a little bit of glory. We even started beating some of the bigger boys in the league again, with memorable home wins over Manchester United, the Scum and Liverpool all happening during his reign.

But the football was as tepid as bath water when the boiler hadn't been on. Plus, you could see that he didn't like playing David Ginola, who was at his peak during Graham's first season in charge.

In the end, it was a regime change that saw off Graham. Not long after an FA Cup quarter-final win at West Ham, the former Gooner was given his marching orders by new owners ENIC, after talking about transfer dealings to the press. A man who was once sacked for being partial to the odd brown paper envelope got another one and ultimately ended his managerial career with us. We never saw higher than 10th in the league at the end of a season and Graham's departure made way for the second coming of Hod.

Glenn Hoddle (2001-03)
Games in charge: 104 (41 wins, 18 draws, 45 defeats)
Win percentage: 39.42%
Highest Premier League finish: 9th

Most memorable moment: Beating Chelsea 5-1 in the Worthington Cup semi-final second leg

Ah, what could have been? Yes, the man who my Father called God (coming from a church warden that's high praise, and brilliantly blasphemous) was back, bringing with him a style of attacking football we hadn't seen for years, and it worked, a bit, for a while.

Strangled by the tight purse strings, Hoddle decided to partner the youngsters he had been forced to play the two months after taking over from Graham (the club had been suffering its annual injury crisis at this point) with experienced free agents such as Teddy Sheringham, Gustavo Poyet and Kasey Keller and the blend of youth and experience came to a head when we thrashed Chelsea 5-1 to reach the Worthington Cup final and put to bed a horrendous hoodoo after a 12-year curse against our rivals.

Sadly though, a patchy performance in the final against Blackburn did for Glenn and Tottenham who for the remainder of his time at the club looked lacking in confidence, ideas and the right players to match his vision.

It all came to an end when a terrible start to our 2003-04 campaign saw us in the bottom half and after nine months of rumours that Hoddle was falling out with his players and even showing some of them up on the training pitch, he was given his marching orders. Like his teammate Ardiles, his reputation as a player with us will always mean that he has a special place in our hearts, even if his time as manager was less than special.

David Pleat (2003-04)
Games in charge: 39 (16 wins, 7 draws, 16 defeats)
Win percentage: 41.03%
Highest Premier League finish: 14th
Most memorable moment: The bloody Manchester City FA Cup game.

Our director of football was no stranger to the role of caretaker at the club. Indeed, he had stepped in twice before with the two previous intermediate periods but this spell was to span almost the length of a season as it became apparent that new chairman Daniel Levy was struggling to convince anybody to come and take over a side who were drifting dangerously towards relegation.

Whilst Pleat managed to keep the club afloat, our former manager was never going to be a permanent recruitment and our players knew it. We struggled for the rest of that season and although we did look quite good in some games, especially when the likes of Robbie Keane, Freddie Kanoute and Jermain Defoe were on form, the side, still containing fragments of the one George Graham had five years previous, needed a massive overhaul.

In the meantime, we were forced to put up with a team who lost 4-3 to Manchester City after being 3-0 up at half-time and which relied on a centre-back partnership of Gary Doherty, who at times was so confidence stricken he didn't even resemble a footballer anymore, and Anthony Gardner.

It was an embarrassing time to be a Spurs fan but in the summer of 2004, we were treated to perhaps the biggest summer of changes we've ever seen in our Premier League years and a hero was to emerge from the clouds surrounding White Hart Lane.

Jacques Santini (2004)
Games in charge: 13 (5 wins, 4 draws, 4 defeats)
Win percentage: 38.46%
Highest Premier League finish: N/A
Most memorable moment: Parking the bus at Stamford Bridge

Not you! Oh okay, fine, I'll write a bit about Jacques Santini then.

Yes, the man to step into the post (finally) was the man who had left the France national team after a disappointing performance at Euro 2004 (they still beat England though, typically) and with him came 22 new players, a whole new management structure and hope that all would be well again at White Hart Lane.

Sadly, this was to be yet another false dawn. Santini's brand of football was boredom on an intergalactic level. Sure, he fixed our defence, with new club captain Ledley King learning from experienced Moroccan acquisition Noureddine Naybet, but we were dull as dishwater going forward.

After just 13 games, Santini quit whilst we were in the middle of a six-game losing streak, leaving us feeling like a joke once again. I saw the breaking news live on Sky Sports News and my jaw nearly smashed through the floor in shock. We seemed to go through managers the way I did football shorts!

Who could we turn to now? Dad, it turned out.

Martin Jol (2004-07)
Games in charge: 148 (67 wins, 38 draws, 43 defeats)
Win percentage: 45.27%
Highest Premier League finish: 5th
Most memorable moment: First win over Chelsea in the league in 26 years

The man who started it all. The progression we saw towards the Champions League final in 2019 truly did begin with Jol, the first manager to lead us back into Europe via the league since the 1980s. Jolly was a popular person and as first team coach (he had always wanted the top job) he stepped up and our brand of football changed overnight. In his second game, we even managed to score four against the old enemy. Sadly, we also conceded five, but Jol's young, exciting dynamic team would finish 5th two seasons in a row and we almost qualified for the Champions League in his first full season.

The likes of Robbie Keane and Ledley King reached their peaks in a team dripping with homegrown talents like Paul Robinson, Aaron Lennon, Jermaine Jenas, Michael Dawson, Michael Carrick, Jermain Defoe, Tom Huddlestone and continental superstars such as Edgar Davids and Dimitar Berbatov.

This was the first Tottenham team I truly fell in love with, with a manager we all loved (he was our first cult boss, with songs like "I Love Martin Jol" and "He's Got No Hair But We Don't Care", and for the first time in the Premier League years we looked like challenging for major honours.

Of course, it all fell apart as Jol fell out with Daniel Levy and Director of Football Damien Comolli and his public sacking in 2007 will never be anything less than scandalous, but we still love him to this day. And he still loves us too.

Juande Ramos (2007-08)
Games in charge: 55 (21 wins, 15 draws, 19 defeats)
Win percentage: 38.18%
Highest Premier League finish: 11th
Most memorable moment: Carling Cup final win in 2008

The man who had won two consecutive UEFA Cup titles with a very well-constructed Sevilla side, Daniel Levy finally got his man in 2007 when the Spaniard Juande Ramos took over following Clive Allen's one-match caretaker role. Ramos's methods were always at odds with a squad who felt that he treated them like children. Then again, he did once allegedly spot some of his players at a McDonalds after training. The ketchup was banned and the players looked leaner and fitter for it (another reason why I could never play football, I love ketchup too much).

Ramos's stricter training drills worked and we beat the Arse in a glorious 5-1 demolition at the Lane taking us towards glory in our 2008 League Cup win over another of our rivals, Chelsea. But the following season Ramos tried to change too much too soon and Robbie Keane, Jermain Defoe, Paul Robinson and Dimitar Berbatov left in the space of two transfer windows.

The replacements in the side struggled to pick up form in the early matches of the 2008-09 season, with Luka Modrić, Heurelho Gomes, David Bentley, Giovanni Dos Santos, Roman Pavlyuchenko and Gilberto all taking a lot of time to find their feet.

In the end, Ramos was cast out after leading us to our worst start to a Premier League season. With two points from eight games, we were in deep, deep trouble and Daniel Levy was left with another managerial change to make.

Harry Redknapp (2008-12)
Games in charge: 198 (98 wins, 50 draws, 50 defeats)
Win percentage: 49.49%
Highest Premier League finish: 4th
Most memorable moment: That first Champions League run in 2010-11

Building on the foundations that Martin Jol had left, 'Arry took us one further in his four years at the club, leading us to the promised land of Champions League football in a memorable and largely enjoyable spell in charge at the Lane.

A cosy arm around the shoulder, a man to get the confidence and the ketchup flowing again and soon after a brilliant 4-4 draw at the Emirates and a late 2-1 win over Liverpool in his first week in charge, we were back up and running.

Redknapp's attacking side was to boast such world-class players as Gareth Bale, who he did nearly sell to Birmingham City for £3m before he turned a corner – and Luka Modrić, plus the surprise deadline day addition of Rafael Van der Vaart. We truly started to compete with the big boys.

His tenure is remembered most fondly for that first Champions League run in which we made it to the quarter-finals, overturning both Milan teams on the way and playing with all the fun and vigour of Tottenham teams of old.

Sadly, though, a court case regarding his tax payments and links to the England job scuppered his chances of challenging for the league in 2011-12 and after early good season form, we ended up slipping to 4th and losing out on Champions League football the following season.

Plus he had to make do with Ryan Nelson and Luis Saha when he wanted Gary Cahill and Eden Hazard and so by summer 2012, Daniel Levy had yet another P45 prepared and 'Arry left with his head held high.

Andre Villas-Boas (2012-13)
Games in charge: 80 (44 wins, 20 draws, 16 defeats)
Win percentage: 55%
Highest Premier League finish: 5th

Most memorable moment: First Premier League win at Old Trafford over Fergie's United since 1989

The first in a trilogy of former Chelsea rejects and easily the most palatable. At 35 years old, Andre Villas-Boas, a former disciple of Bobby Robson and Josè Mourinho, joined us following a reputation-tarnishing season at Chelsea, where he failed to tame the bigger characters and became our youngest coach in the Premier League era.

Yet in his only full season, AVB went a long way to putting it back together as Spurs finished with a record points tally up to that point (72) and missed out on Champions League football again with one point. He brought in players who would become integral to our side for the rest of the decade in Hugo Lloris, Mousa Dembele and Jan Vertonghen and was at the helm when Gareth Bale went truly supernova.

With a more conservative approach than his predecessor, AVB still managed to get the best out of a team that lost Ledley King, Rafael Van der Vaart and Luka Modrić the previous summer and even after Bale followed Modrić to Madrid, things still looked rosey after we signed the Magnificent Seven.

Trouble was brewing behind the scenes. Key targets identified by AVB were not purchased by Levy and ENIC and interruption from new Director of Football Franco Baldini led to tensions. The young boss was also at odds with the press, who stoked the flames when he claimed that the White Hart Lane faithful shouldn't be so quick to turn on the team when times got hard.

In the end, we had our arses handed to us several times by the teams that we wanted to compete with and after a horror show during a 5-0 home loss to Liverpool, AVB was no more.

He's still our most successful manager in the Prem years in win percentage, so despite a less-than-buccaneering playing style, he wasn't as bad as some of us remember.

Tim Sherwood (2013-14)
Games in charge: 28 (14 wins, 4 draws, 10 defeats)
Win percentage: 50%
Highest Premier League finish: 6th
Most memorable moment: Handing his Gillet to a fan and inviting him to sit in his seat

You have to hand it to Tim Sherwood, he could talk the talk. He must do considering he did enough to let Daniel Levy give him an 18-month contract to take over as Head Coach after spending several years working with the development squads. We bore the fruits of his labours down there too as youth team products Nabil Bentaleb and Harry Kane made themselves first-team regulars after impressing.

But the same problems that saw the downfall of his predecessor saw the downfall of Sherwood also. Players drifting in and out of form, including a number of the seven signings in the summer and we were truly outclassed any time we came up against our rivals for the top 4. He did get the best out of Emmanuel Adebayor, who had an Indian summer during the season, but the fans were far from happy.

And yet Sherwood still won half his games, which considering he had nowhere near the same level of experience as some of the others on this list is very impressive and slightly mad. He was tactically naive at times, and the players didn't like him after his moody outburst after a 4-0 defeat against Chelsea.

We'd drifted further away from our goal of staying in touch with the leading pack and Sherwood's contract was terminated a day after Ledley King's testimonial game in May 2014, a game that he was invited to play in but declined to, probably because getting booed every time he'd have touched the ball would have taken the piss.

Mauricio Pochettino (2014-2019)
Games in charge: 293 (159 wins, 62 draws, 72 defeats)
Win percentage: 54.27%
Highest Premier League finish: 2nd
Most memorable moment: Ajax.

Of all the names on this list, Mauricio Pochettino is probably the one who promised the least and yet delivered the most. His arrival saw a muffled applause from fans who had been through the emotional wringer a few years before and after a few months it looked like the Argentine's appointment was just another poor choice from Daniel Levy. But Harry Kane's deflected free-kick winner against Aston Villa in the last minute of a difficult game was a sliding-doors moment.

Having inherited a large number of the Sherwood squad, Poch began to turf out many of the old guard, such as Michael Dawson, Younes Kaboul, Aaron Lennon, Emmanuel Adebayor and the big signings that hadn't worked in Paulinho and Roberto Soldado. Poch constructed a young, hungry side who, despite losing the Carling Cup final 2-0 to Josè Mourinho's streetwise Chelsea side, went from strength to strength, with us challenging for the title not once but twice.

We finished third, then second, having gained 86 points and had a side full of world-class players again. He took us into the Champions League, where Poch's defining moment came in Amsterdam in 2019, where we all know what happened.

My only gripe with Poch, until he joined Chelsea in 2023, that is, was that he was openly dismissive of the FA and League Cups. At a time when Spurs were accused of bottling it when the going got tough, a more serious attitude to winning these trophies would have set us up for so much more.

Alas, it wasn't to be. Poch was sacked after a difficult start to the 2019-20 season, a year after he'd gone 18 months without signing anybody, seen us play at Wembley when we were homeless, the transition into the new stadium and of course the Champions League final. It was a bittersweet ride but in the end, I wouldn't have missed it for the world.

Josè Mourinho (2019-21)
Games in charge: 86 (44 wins, 19 draws, 23 defeats)
Win percentage: 51.16%
Highest Premier League finish: 6th
Most memorable moment: Beating rival Pep Guardiola's Man City side with a weakened side 2-0

When you've been oh so close to the summit without tasting the glory, it makes sense to go out and get a specialist in winning trophies and Josè was just that. The only issue was that, yes, he was another Chelsea and after we had witnessed his implosion in charge of Manchester United, we all knew that the same would happen at the Tottenham Hotspur Stadium.

But Josè's time was beset with issues inside and outside the game. Key players reaching the end of their peak, injuries and then a global pandemic lumped right into the middle. Plus we never really took to him. It was always an uneasy marriage between the two of us. We only really wanted the Special One to get us over the line with a trophy and most of us were willing to sacrifice our brand of football to do so. At times it looked like finally, we were about to get that monkey off our back, but after a slide down the table, players falling out with him and the situation around the club becoming toxic, Josè was given his marching orders just days before a major final. To me, I felt like the whole appointment had been pointless. If you bring in a guy who is renowned for winning things, why would you sack him the week of a final? Were things really that bad?

He said later on that Spurs is the only club he feels no affection for. This is funny because a lot of fans would say that the feeling is mutual.

Nuno Espirito Santo (2021)
Games in charge: 17 (8 wins, 2 draws, 7 defeats)
Win percentage: 47.06%
Highest Premier League finish: N/A
Most memorable moment: Opening day win over Man City

Remember when he said he'd make us proud? Me too, unfortunately.

Nuno's stay at Spurs was thankfully short. He did have some good moments, however. An opening-day victory over Manchester City and two 1-0 victories over Wolves and Watford saw the Portuguese win the season's first Manager of the Month Award. He had done it all whilst navigating the Harry Kane situation, following the England striker being tapped up by Sky, sorry, I mean Manchester City and wanting out.

But like a house of cards, it all crumbled and after ten games and five defeats in the league, Nuno knew the writing was on the wall when the boo boys came. During a woeful 3-0 defeat at home to Manchester United, he took off the popular Lucas Moura for Steven Bergwijn. The fans didn't like it, boos ran around the stadium and Nuno's P45 was in the post.

Antonio Conte (2021-23)
Games in charge: 77 (41 wins, 12 draws, 24 defeats)
Win percentage: 53.25%
Highest Premier League finish: 4th
Most memorable moment: His press conference meltdown

It was good, while it lasted. Well, some of it. That blinding win over the Gooners in May, when we won 3-0, felt amazing. And the final day when we beat them to fourth place when we dished out wallops in Norwich 5-0 and Sonny won the Golden Boot. And Rodrigo Bentancur and Dejan Kulusevski coming over from Italy and being immense for us. And what about that comeback against Leicester too? Amazing scenes and a game that means Steven Bergwijn will forever stay in our hearts.

But Christ, if Josè Mourinho was the warm-up for a lesson in toxicity, Antonio Conte was the real master in spurstaneous combustion. He always seemed to be talking about leaving, as he was only on an 18-month contract, and his early outburst after a 1-0 defeat to Burnley in February, just four months into his reign, was a sign of things to come. It was fully expected though.

Not content with how the Josè appointment went, Daniel Levy gave it another go with a man more explosive, more likely to throw his toys out of the pram if he didn't give his way and expected different results. Conte was our third ex-Chelsea appointment in a decade (fourth if you want to go back to Hoddle), the only one to get us into the Champions League, for the first time in three seasons.

In the summer he complained about the influx of players, saying that the club had made club signings. Then the Italian suffered a triple bereavement and a dodgy gall bladder. His Director of Football was banned and by the time the game finished 3-3 against Southampton in March, in his final press conference as manager was a man signing his own resignation letter.

Ange Postecoglou (2023-?)
Games in charge: 41 (21 wins, 7 draws, 13 defeats)
Win percentage: 51.22%
Highest Premier League finish: 5th
Most memorable moment: "I'm just copying Pep, mate."

The latest man to lead us in the Premier League era and the incumbent at the time of writing (knowing our luck it'll have all gone tits up before the start of the season and Levy will have pulled the trigger again!) So far, the popular Australian has given us our attacking football back with a promising young side led by new team captain Heung-Min Son. It's too early to draw too many conclusions but I've liked what I've seen.

He also seems to have charmed those in the media, having Neville and Carragher act like little school boys around him on Sky Sports and we've got a song for him in Angels, via some tweaked Robbie Williams lyrics (the video of the singer himself singing our version went viral instantly).

The jury will be out until we win something under Big Ange or he becomes the latest false dawn but home wins against Manchester United and Liverpool, impressive draws against the Scum and Man City and a fantastic first ten games all bode well for the manager's philosophy. We went unbeaten in the first ten games but criticisms so far include not dealing with conceding from set pieces, not adapting enough, the 5 defeats in seven games at the end of the season and getting in completely wrong with the fans in that weird game against Manchester City, which we wanted to lose to mean that it would result in the Scum not winning the title. Hopefully, he will add some squad depth in the summer and get rid of the last bits of deadwood and the future will be bright.

Please, for the love of God, let it be bright!

SECOND HALF

THE WORST OF TIMES

8

WORST SEASONS

In the 32 years since the Premier League was formed, Tottenham have thrown at us some truly appalling moments. Short of actually getting relegated, I'm not so sure that a club can go through the wringer as much as we have. We've had food poisoning on the final day, other clubs winning trophies and then instantly knocking us out of competitions the following season, and that's just the good seasons!

I loathe to include the endless times that players have simply given up on the pitch, managers have given up on the training ground or had a full-blown mental breakdown in a press conference and embarrassing results that have been but the shitty cherry on the turd cake. Alas, I can't ignore them. We as Spurs fans have learned to take the rough with the smooth and on that subject, not all of these seasons were total tripe for there are some nuggets of gold in the muddy slurry that is our worst years in the Prem. So let me get my hands dirty and recall some for you...

1993/94 - Ardiles takes over, Sheringham gets injured a lot and Spurs are nearly relegated

Thankfully I'm a little too young for the second season of the Premier League, and looking back all I'm relieved that I was. Those of you who are younger than thirty will struggle to remember a time when Tottenham not so much flirted with the prospect of relegation but full-on French kissed it. Sure, the infamous "two points from eight games" scenario was brought into terrifying reality by Juande Ramos in 2008 but that was but a hiccup before results took an upward turn.

But back in 1994, in the days when the top tier of English football included 22 teams, Spurs won just four home games in the league. Four. All to sides who finished 16th and lower in the table (Everton, Oldham, Southampton and Manchester City). We finished 15th, to this day our lowest-ever finish, just three points better off than Sheffield United, who did admittedly have a much worse goal difference than our –5. But after finishing a positive 8th in the inaugural Premier League season, how was it all going so wrong?

As it normally is with Spurs, any sign of positive forward momentum can be halted within an instant and the catalyst for this turmoil started at the end of the previous campaign. Chairman Alan Sugar took the unpopular decision to sack manager and now Chief Executive Terry Venables. Players were up in arms. PFA Player of the Year Teddy Sheringham spoke about how upset the players were at El Tel's dismissal on national TV. Neil "Razor" Ruddock's wife paraded outside Sugar's mansion with a placard cleverly stating that Spurs wanted, "T, no Sugar." Imagine Christian Romero's missus doing the same thing now!

Ruddock himself, having only returned to the club the previous summer for his second stay in N17, ultimately left to join Liverpool, as did club stalwart Paul Allen and twelve games into the season Gordon Durie. Whilst Venables and Sugar battled in the High Court, the chairman needed to make a positive appointment to get both players and fans back on side.

By this time, some of the men who were at the heart of Tottenham's last successful period had begun to find their feet in management. Glenn Hoddle, who had already agreed on a gentleman's handshake with Chelsea chairman Ken Bates, turned down the opportunity to rejoin his boyhood club as player/manager. Osvaldo Ardiles, on the other hand, was only too keen to come back to the club where he won an FA Cup and UEFA Cup a decade earlier. The popular Argentine was joined in the dugout by club legend and all-time appearance maker Steve Perryman and the two led Spurs into the new season at Newcastle United, the club Ardiles had managed a season before last, having spent the intermediate time in charge of West Bromwich Albion. New boys Colin Calderwood – Ruddock's replacement – and Jason Dozzell, who joined from Swindon and Ipswich respectively, played much of the campaign and it looked like Ardile's new-look attacking Tottenham might be onto something. By mid-October, Spurs had won five, drawn three and lost two league games (one of those a rarer than a shiny Charizard Pokemon card or a unicorn that runs on water win at Anfield over

Liverpool), sitting 7th in the league, looking up. What could go wrong?

Well, pretty much everything. First our talisman and best player Sheringham suffered his worst season yet with injuries (although he still managed 13 league goals in 19 outings, so thank Christ he wasn't out for longer!) and during a winless streak of nine games, Ardiles attacking tactics came into question. The seven matches lost on the bounce from January to March plunged Spurs towards the precipice of Division One. True, the football was entertaining..., but the cohesion between what was a blunted attack, and a defence that sometimes included David Kerslake, Kevin Scott and Stuart Nethercott, was steadfast as a wet wipe in the wind and many wondered if the World Cup winner had gone a bit mad.

But Spurs were shipping goals for fun and finding it hard to replace their fallen hero. New signing Ronnie Rosenthal, famous to English fans for his glaring open goal miss whilst playing for Liverpool against Aston Villa the previous season, only managed two goals in 16 games. A midfield surplus of Darren Anderton, Steve Sedgeley, Darren Caskey, Vinnie Samways, Nick Barmby and Jason Dozzell did their best to find goals where they could, with Dozzell managing to almost reach double figures in the league with nine making him the best of a toiling bunch. Growing up in the 90s and early 00s I was always left to believe that Dozzell was a real flop for us but the stats do not lie. It wouldn't be until Gareth Bale seventeen years later that another midfielder would best Dozzell's goalscoring feats that season and register double figures in the league for us.

But in truth, he just didn't have the names to play the system he wanted. In short, when Sheringham wasn't playing, the Spurs were in big trouble. They won only one more home game between October and the end of the season in May and failed to win any back-to-back games until a glorious two-match running streak at the end of March/early April and Sheringham's return coincided with the club inching its way to safety.

Luckily for all involved, the England striker was back for the run-in and after crucial wins against fellow strugglers Everton and Norwich City (who this season beat Bayern Munich in the UEFA Cup) Spurs' form tanked yet again in April, as the Hammers beat us 4-1 on our home turf, Coventry then narrowly beat us 1-0 and Leeds put us to the sword 2-0.

It was thanks to a 3-0 tonking of Southampton, complete with a rare clean sheet, and a penultimate game away victory against condemned Oldham Athletic in which Samways and David Howells steered Tottenham to mathematical safety in a nervy 2-1 win. It astonishes me that this one isn't talked about more. We of a certain vintage crow about Klinsmann's four goals against Wimbledon, and for good reason, but the 1993-94 season final round of fixtures was extraordinary because, although Swindon Town were well adrift at the foot of the table, anyone out of five clubs could have gone down. A final-day defeat at home to Wimbledon could have seen us down instead of Sheffield United and the recently vanquished Oldham.

But the bad news was about to get worse for Spurs fans as the club was punished by the FA for financial irregularities during the previous chairman Irving Scholar's time at the club, with a 12-point deduction the following season, a ban from the FA Cup and a £600,000 fine, for a club who survived relegation by the skin of their teeth. The writing was on the wall. Spurs were in deep trouble and needed something special to inject the club with positive energy and optimism.

Thankfully, they got it...

1996-97 – Bland kits, bland football, injuries galore and mid-table obscurity

1995-96 had been a relatively positive season for the lilywhites. Despite finishing 8th, one place lower than in the Jürgen Klinsmann-inspired campaign the previous year, Spurs were unlucky not to qualify for Europe, losing out on goal difference as they occupied two other sides on 61 points. New boy Chris Armstrong had also forged a lethal partnership with Teddy Sheringham, with both marksmen scoring 46 goals between them in all competitions. After the departures of Klinsmann, Gica Popescu and Nick Barmby, the team had come together and performed admirably. Even the defence was looking more assured with ever-present Ian Walker cementing his first team place after sharing the gloves with Erik Thorsvedt for a few years previously and even keeping seven clean sheets in a row in the league. I had to re-read that statistic several times before typing.

1996 was also the season in which football came home and the exciting Euro 96 was still fresh in our minds where Sheringham and Darren Anderton had featured in every England game as the Three Lions were so, so close to winning the tournament. There was a strong Spurs contingent in Terry Venables' squad that summer, with Ian Walker and NAME REDACTED also included and Gerry Francis must have been purring to have them back in the spine of his Spurs side and with the additions of Denmark international Allan Nielsen and QPR veteran Clive Wilson (yes, our transfers were not of great quality as back then we signed oldies instead of true goldies), Spurs appeared to have a squad to try and go one better than the campaign before.

How wrong we were.

On the opening day, although we ran out 2-0 winners thanks to a double from Armstrong, the tone was set for what was to dog Spurs for the entire season. Yes, the footballing Gods decided to dish out to Tottenham players injuries much in the same vein Oprah Winfrey gives away free prizes. Firstly, Gary Mabbutt broke his leg in the 18th minute. Then in the second home game of the season, a 0-0 draw with Everton, Armstrong was to succumb to the first of many absences in his Tottenham career. And then just as in previous seasons, the linchpin to all that was good about Tottenham was also crocked. Teddy Sheringham, who was closing in on five seasons and 100 goals for Spurs, only managed seven in the entire campaign, his lowest return in a lilywhite shirt. Without the frontmen, Francis had to call on youngster

Rory Allen to lead the attack in the early months of the campaign but again we looked hopeless. Goals were also becoming a problem at the other end and so Francis looked to Europe and signed Ramon Vega from Grasshoppers for £3.75m to help shore things up at the back. Why Gerry and his trademark mullet thought that signing Ramon Vega may improve the defence I'll never know as the Swiss international always looked suspect to me and my very young eyes at this point.

By Christmas, we'd also picked up this really exciting Norwegian kid called Steffen Iversen. He was blonde, like Klinsmann, played up front like Klinsmann and came from abroad just like, well, you get the picture. Since Jürgen's time, foreign imports had become all the rage in the Premier League. Sadly, whilst that lot seemed to be shopping in all the right places, we were picking up ours in those back-alley souvenir shops that copy your credit card. For all the early promise that Iversen showed, and he did score a corking hat-trick up at Roker Park against Sunderland, he still looked raw in a side that at this point was starting to look a little overdone.

In the end, we finished tenth but take a look at the Premier League table from that year and you'd be forgiven for thinking we'd been rather middling in our results. However, Middlesborough, who suffered a real Jekyll and Hyde year having lost both League and FA Cup finals to the same team (I don't have the stomach to mention who it was), boasted the likes of Fabrizio Ravenelli, Juninho and Emerson and were relegated on 41! Considering we survived on 46 points, with the crap we had in our side then, I think should have counted ourselves pretty lucky!

I'd await our inclusion on Match of the Day with eager intent on Sunday mornings whilst I was wolfing down my breakfast, only to see us often as one of the final games. Back in the days before every match was afforded a full highlights package, if you were one of the least glamorous ties you'd be lucky to get just the goals shown or a few chances that had gone awry as was normally the case and the glorious tones of Gerald Sinstadt. The only other occasion I'd see us was if we were playing one of the big boys. However, this was back in the days when we got spanked every time we faced them. Okay, we did beat United 4-1 at home the previous year but this was the season when all of that started to happen. The Scum did us over in a year when some speccy twirp called Arsène Wenger had come in and made them look great again. The Chelski hoodo was alive and strong and you could bet that if a side had the slightest sniff of European qualification we'd be in trouble but the truly worst moment of the campaign came against Newcastle. Do you think we have a bad recent history up on Tyneside? Try being demolished 7-1. I felt like Matthew McConaughey in Interstellar when he watched the home movies of times he missed with his children as Teletext kept blinking the updates. By the end, I was a husk. How could they do it to me? My Dad must have seen the look in my eyes and recognised it immediately as a bad Spurs result. I consoled myself in my Beano comics and Doctor Who videos thinking to myself that being a Spurs fan wasn't as fun as I thought it was going to be.

My enduring memory of this season is of the final day. We were playing Coventry, who needed a result to confirm their Premiership status for the following campaign. There was personal pride on the line here, not just for the boys from White Hart Lane, but for me too. My Uncle and cousin were massive Cov fans and considering the Sky Blues needed to beat us to stay up, the battle lines were drawn. Thank God I was too young for a mobile phone and that social media was just a mere glint in Mark Zuckerburg's eye at the time because, yes, you guessed it, Coventry turned up and did a number on us as we went down 2-1 in front of a disgruntled home support.

I've heard eyewitness accounts of fans ripping up their season tickets (fair enough, it was the last game of the season) and throwing them onto the pitch at the players as they embarked on what must have been an embarrassing lap of shame.

Meanwhile, in the Gribble household, it was enough to pull the telephone line from the wall and make excuses for every family gathering that summer.

I remember watching Dion Dublin et al celebrating on Match of the Day and almost feeling jealous of Coventry. At least they had something to celebrate come the end of the season. Us? Nothing. And that is a shameful feeling for an eight-year-old to possess. No one should feel jealous of Coventry!

As the players walked down the tunnel of an almost empty White Hart Lane, the hangers-on either being enraged fans or those taking pity on them, it must have dawned on Gerry Francis that he was on borrowed time. Yes, he could blame the injuries (don't worry, he did). Yes, he had used a whopping 33 players in competitive games across the campaign in a desperate bid to find a winning side but the harsh reality was that in the space of nine months, we'd fallen backwards, closer in points to Division One than we were to title winners Manchester United.

Still, at least we had Teddy...

1997-98 – Another relegation scrap, Klinsmann and Ginola give us hope and that bloody train ticket.

Whoops, I spoke too soon. It wasn't long before Alex Ferguson, before the knighthood but after the Fergie time infamy, had swooped in and plucked our very own Teddy from our toy box. Sheringham, despite his injuries the previous year, was arguably in his prime and his £3.5m transfer to Old Trafford was gut-wrenching but Fergie wanted a replacement for Eric Cantona and ultimately, as what normally happened back then, he got his way and Teddy was a Spur no more. I'm still angry that Francis couldn't have offered them Rosenthal or Vega instead but there you go.

But all was not lost because Alan Sugar had just the thing to help the bitter medicine go down. He went out and bought two Newcastle players and considering they had all but ground us into the dirt last year and helped the Magpies finish second two years running, I thought this was a sensation. He'd only gone and got us Sir Les Bloody Ferdinand and David Bloody Ginola! I was cock-a-hoop. I thought we'd win the league! I even told a couple of friends of mine at school. Les Ferdinand and David Ginola. Wow. I mean yes, one of them was a little past his prime and the other had a tendency to fall to the ground rather theatrically but they were ours and they were quality! Add to that the addition of winger Josè Dominguez, with the diminutive stature of Richard Hammond, from Sporting Lisbon and we looked exciting. Who cares if Sheringham had gone? We had the real deal now.

Sure, we lost the opening-day fixture against Manchester United 2-0. Vega was as useless as usual, putting through his own net after going missing in the build-up to the opener from Nicky Butt but at least Teddy Sheringham, stung by the chorus of boos every time he touched the ball, showed that he still cared by missing a penalty. Anyone can lose their first game, especially against the champions but we had 37 more to eclipse them.

But for all my early season optimism 1997-98 was yet another nightmare in the life of a Spurs fan in the nineties. My excitement soon turned to abject sorrow as Spurs, just like their kit manufacturer at the time, were pony. We finished 14th, on 44 points just 4 points above Bolton Wanderers who sunk into Division One. It heralded the first managerial change in my memory as Gerry Francis, who tended to look down at the floor during interviews on Football Focus and Match of the Day, was given his marching orders not long after a 4-0 drubbing at Anfield. Following the appointment of them down the road of Arsène Wenger, we went out and got our mysterious foreign coach in the hope of the same level of success that they were about to embark on. But Sugar, not long after saying, "You're fired," to Francis, then said "You're hired" to a man whose entire stay at Tottenham would be summed up by one train ticket and one press conference. Christian Gross.

It's a sad indicator of how far we had fallen at this time that we had to start measuring our misery against the success that the Gooners began to have this season. Before Wenger arrived Arsenal's years in the Prem were just as barren as ours. Sure, they had won a couple of trophies in recent memory, but then so had we. But David Dein's hiring of Wenger turned the tide and the Frenchman...well you know all the rest. I grit my teeth as I write this but he revolutionised not just English football but the Scum to glorious new heights. It was this season that they would win the double. The only double we got all season was when we played the same team twice and they beat us, twice. And Gross, for all his credentials in his native Switzerland and the success he had there later on, was a terrible fit for us and ever since then, I can never trust Alan Sugar when he appoints someone on The Apprentice.

Back to way back when and by Christmas we were in trouble. Big trouble. Despite a confident 3-0 defeat over fellow strugglers Barnsley, featuring a double from Ginola, it was all going wrong. Having not sat higher than ninth all season, we were now languishing in the bottom three. There was even the result against Chelsea, who despite being 1-1 at the break, had clicked into gear with their wealth of foreign talent and destroyed us 6-1 at full-time. At home. Near

Christmas. I can still hear my Dad's disbelieving cry of, "THEY BEAT US 6-1!!!" as the videprinter revealed the scores on Grandstand. It shook the very foundations of the football core that ran through us. I didn't know what to do except laugh at the futility of it all.

Sir Les wasn't scoring. He'd been out injured a lot. Ginola had Paul Mahorn and Neale Fenn to cross to. Iversen and Armstrong couldn't get a run in this side to help due to injuries and our defence was changing with so much alarming frequency for one reason or another that I swear I saw young rookie Stephen Clemence play left back on more than one occasion. And we had John Scales, and a beyond past it Gary Mabbutt trying to shore things up. It was like all the holes in the cheese from Switzerland had been brought over too by Gross. There was a 4-1 thrashing by Aston Villa, 3-0 to Leicester and 4-0 away to Coventry. It was insufferable.

We were doomed.

Gross acted quickly and the festive period gave us a little bit of cheer as Jürgen Klinsmann rejoined from Sampdoria. Some saw it as a superficial bid for the German legend to get fit for the World Cup in France the following summer after falling out of favour in Italy, and some also bemoaned the fact that the veteran striker was well past his best. He wasn't the only old import from Italy that Winter as Italy midfielder Nicola Berti – proud owner of a wonderful barnet that still gets sung about on the terraces occasionally today! - was prized away on a free transfer from Inter Milan. You'd be forgiven that Gross would be looking to recruit at the back and yes, he did plump for Chelsea reserve goalkeeper Frode Grodas to support the struggling Walker and youngster Espen Baardsen but the only other signing was Moussa Saib from Valencia. The midfielder had turned down the Gooners the previous summer and was now lining up in a side who were about the embark on a great escape.

Klinsmann initially struggled and it took nearly a month before he opened his account for the season with a deft finish against West Ham to beat our London rivals 1-0 and two weeks later we blasted Blackburn Rovers aside 3-0 thanks to goals from Berti, Armstrong and Ruel Fox in the best performance of the season to date. Performances seemed to be improving just at the right time as the experienced heads in the side began to make a mark. Between February and the end of the season, we only lost three in 14 games and the team began to find confidence and consistency. With an entertaining 3-3 home draw against Liverpool followed by a 2-0 win over Newcastle thanks to goals from Klinsmann and Sir Les, with Sicknote back in the side just in time to stake his claim in the England squad for the World Cup, it all came down to the penultimate game in a difficult encounter with Wimbledon at Selhurst Park.

We started brightly in the late Spring sunshine, all white kit glimmering just like my hopes that this was the day that we secured Premiership survival. It started brilliantly too, with Les Ferdinand scoring for the second game in a row and poking us in the lead. However, the joy didn't last long as from out of nowhere Peter Fear hit a half volley from range that sailed into the bottom corner. Then the inevitable disaster happened. Fear scored again, this time a volley from an acute angle inside the box. A massive effort was needed to save our season and thankfully Ginola twisted and turned on the wing and put in a low cross for Jürgen the German to stab home.

By the second half, we began to truly run away with it and Klinsmann scored another three goals, his four in the match doubling his tally for the season but more importantly consolidating our place in the top flight for another season. He even had time to set up Saib for a sixth as we ran out 6-2 victors, and that was that, we were safe!

I don't recall where I was on that day. I reckon I was probably hiding under a cushion or something, however I do remember seeing the goals on MOTD and feeling great that we hadn't gone down. A dead rubber at home to Southampton concluded a nightmare of a season for us as Klinsmann signed off his career with us with a superb volley and Gary Mabbutt appeared for the 611th and last time as after 16 years he was hanging up his boots. It was sad to see two stalwarts of my years as a fan go, especially Klinsmann who without him and his dive celebration a few years earlier might not have spurred me on to be a lilywhite.

Looking back now, in the last years of the 20th century, as New Labour and Cool Brittania ruled the waves and Hoddle and the boys marched on to France to bring the World Cup home for England, it was a funny old season. Much changed and yet nothing did at the same time. For all the faces coming and going at Spurs, on the pitch and behind the scenes, we had become a team stuck in the mid-table mire. Sometimes seasons like 1997-98 pop up on YouTube for a bit and if you're ever down in the dumps over a recent result I implore you to watch it. To quote a popular song of the time, "We've come a long, long way together…"

2000-01 – Sugar departs, ENIC arrive and the bloke in the raincoat is sacked before a NLD Semi-final.

You'd be forgiven for thinking that at the turn of the millennium, things might have just started to turn a corner for our friends in lilywhite and from the outset it did look like something might have been changing. For starters, chairman Alan Sugar (yes, that one off the tele, younger readers) had put his money in his pocket and spent big on £11m Ukranian striker Sergei Rebrov from Dynamo Diev.

The talented forward had impressed alongside his compatriot and strike partner Andrei Shevchenko in the Champions League the previous season and at 26, looked just the kind of signing we needed. With his peak surely a few years off and his record of 139 goals in 283 games for the Ukranian side, fans like me were drooling at the prospect of Rebrov tearing up the league and propelling us towards Europe.

Unfortunately, the other two pre-season signings were a little more underwhelming. After a decade of picking the ball out of the net and putting his hands on his hips in annoyance, Ian Walker was finally replaced between the sticks by Neil Sullivan, a free transfer from relegated rivals Wimbledon. Not to do Sullivan a disservice but this was the same man who had been chipped from the halfway line by David Beckham a few years previously and who had failed to dislodge geriatric goalkeeper Jim Leighton from between the sticks in the World Cup in France in 1998. He was followed to the Lane by teammate left-back Ben Thatcher for a dizzying £5m. Whatever Sugar was smoking back then it must have been off because although the club needed back-up for Mauricio Tarrico, Thatcher didn't seem like the answer.

To compound Spurs' estimations of a successful season for a change, David Ginola was sold to Aston Villa for £3m. At 33 years of age, but a mere spring chicken compared to some of the other aged players at the club at the time, the French maverick was indeed past his peak but he was also the only creative spark in an otherwise dour team back then. True he was old. And now I understand where manager George Graham and the board were coming from on this one but at the time it felt gut-wrenching to see the man who had been our hero for the last few years carted off.

There was also the impending storm of what was going on with club captain NAME REDACTED. The local boy had expressed his wish to lift more silverware following our 1999 Worthington Cup triumph and had just entered the final year of his contract. Despite giving sound bites to the press early on that he would be staying, Judas was keeping his cards close to his chest and the club in the dark as to what was going to happen next.

So, in hindsight, the first full season of the 21st century looked like it promised a glimmer of hope that Spurs could do something special, especially since the year ended in a one and Tottenham always won a trophy when the year ends in one, that was lucky, right? Chas and Dave hadn't been lying to me, had they?

What followed was nine months of upheaval, terrible football and an injury list longer than War and Peace. In the Premier League, we finished eleventh, the shit sandwich between Newcastle, who also endured an injury-ravaged season and Leicester City, who had completely fallen off a cliff following their shocking FA Cup Quarter-final defeat to lower league Tranmere Rovers. They still found time to beat us in the penultimate game of the season though, so they had that at least...

We just couldn't find a settled first eleven that season. If you look back at the team that we had it was full of mature heads and raw as mooing meat youngsters. We seemed to have accumulated several professionals who if they had been four or five years younger could have driven us towards some form of glory, but there were just too many players on the wrong side of thirty and they seemed to get injured. A lot.

Take our forward line, for instance. Although Les Ferdinand was a legendary player in England he was pushing 35 at the end of the season and with a decent appearance return of 28 league games this season – his most by a long shot since joining the club in the summer of 1997 – he did his best but still had moments where his form fell off a cliff. Then there was Chris Armstrong. A decent signing – indeed a club record signing when he replaced Jürgen Klinsmann in 1995 – but only managed two goals and rarely featured. He also made a point of never celebrating, a reaction to years of fans who had derided him for not being as good as Heir Jürgen had been. Then there was Steffen Iversen. If you don't know who he was and can't put a name to his face, think of how Gordon Ramsay would have looked in his early twenties and you don't even need to Google him. The Norwegian was young and had a promising year the season before, but only managed two goals in 14 games. Things got so bad that one festive fixture away to newly promoted Ipswich Town heralded no fit strikers and so utility man Gary Doherty was partnered up front with fellow injury merchant, winger Willem Korsten. We lost, unsurprisingly considering Ipswich shocked the league that season and finished 5th, and looked toothless and old in places so often this season we were like a care home with a denture shortage.

As much as I loved him, poor Darren Anderton wasn't seen in a first-team game after February. Tim Sherwood and Steffen Freund, the arthritic heartbeat in this tired team, were also out most of the campaign. Even Stephen Carr, who back then was amazing, seemed to lose his fitness for a bit and simultaneously his hair. We spent months Oyvind Leonhardsen-less and had to make do with the likes of Gary Doherty, Stephen Clemence, Ledley King, Matt Etherington, Anthony Gardner, Luke Young, Alton Thelwell and Simon Davies to fill in as and when. To their credit, they weren't bad and it was exciting to see these youngsters get a go, but it did seem like it was too soon to blood so many youngsters at once. Like slaves to the lions, they marched out week-on-week, giving it their best but ending up ripped open at the end. They needed a helping hand and despite wins at home against Liverpool and Manchester United on the final day of the season, there were very few highlights.

It also turned out that the signing of Rebrov wasn't the answer to our goalscoring prayers. He managed a fairly middling 12 goals in all competitions and finished as our top scorer unsurprisingly, but a never-ending merry-go-round of strikers from the treatment table and lack of creativity behind him hampered his settlement. He also looked a little lightweight for the famously bullish Premier League at the time. In the cold light of day though things didn't look good. We failed to score in 16 of our 38 Premier League games, including a sequence of four dreary 0-0 results in January. We won 13 games, lost 15 and drew 10 with a minus 7 goal difference from 47 scored to 54 conceded.

But back then it didn't matter so much if you had an off-year in the league as long as you did well in the cups and Spurs...well...we gave it our best shot. Not in the League Cup, mind, where we succumbed to Division One side and eventual finalists Birmingham City at home 3-1 but the FA Cup, now that had our name on it. Everyone said it. Well, Mark Lawrenson did on Football Focus and I took that as gospel and when you've scrapped by the third round with a last-minute Gary Doherty header against lowly Leyton

Orient, then you've come back at The Valley against a good Charlton Athletic side from two goals down to win 4-2, you just got the feeling it might be our year. Hell, even a win over West Ham, that's West Ham with the likes of Frank Lampard, Michael Carrick, Joe Cole, Paulo Di Canio and alike, at Upton Park too, and now we were in a semi-final against Arsenal.

It felt like mere hours after the ref had blown his final whistle that boredom merchant George Graham was given his marching orders by new owners ENIC, who had taken over from Alan Sugar officially in March. The only man to have led the club to silverware since Terry Venables' Tottenham had overcome Nottingham Forest in the FA Cup in 1991, had complained in the press about the club's transfer dealings and had duly received his P45 with haste. To be fair to the man in the raincoat, I too would have bemoaned the club's dealings back then to anyone who would have listened. £5m man Ben Thatcher hadn't lit up the Lane and had been injured most of the season so really, who could blame him?

This dramatic event, just days before the biggest game of our season, did pave the way however for hope in the form of Hoddle. Yes, Glenn the Messiah returned as boss and everything started to feel rosey again. Even I felt compelled that week in the build-up to that massive cup tie to make a Spurs pencil case in my Textiles class at school. However, our performance in that game fell apart at the seams, just like said pencil case.

As Iversen's wayward volley smashed an unaware Doherty in the face and sailed past David Seaman in the 14th minute at Old Trafford, I nearly put a hole through the floor jumping around my bedroom. We'd been outplayed and yet here we were, 76 minutes from the FA Cup final! My Dad, too nervous to listen in to the game on my little radio, bounced up the stairs and burst into my room. 'Doherty's scored, Dad!' I yelled. His look of delight soon fell. 'It's too early,' he said and like Eeyore from Winnie the Pooh, he trudged from my room and back downstairs.

He was right. Minutes later NAME RADACTED committed a foul in a dangerous area and had Gazza'd himself in the process. It was his final act as a Spurs player, except for driving a skewer through our collective hearts, that is. From the resultant free-kick, Patrick Vieira towered above Chris Perry, a defender so small he'd have made Diego Maradona look like Peter Crouch, to give the Gooners a deserved equaliser.

They ended up winning. Of course they did, and I had to try my best to hold back the tears when I walked past our Arsenal-supporting neighbour's house as the little girl who lived there screamed, 'We beat you!' from her bedroom window.

It was a depressing year and yet as Glenn Hoddle was back, Spurs would surely be a force again. As the curtain shut on yet another awful year as a Spurs fan, the future looked bright...for a week or two at least. It wasn't the last time our loathsome North London rivals bettered us that season.

Yes, Judas did the dirty on us and when his contract was up, he was off to Highbury. Bastard.

2002/03 - Keano joins, Rivaldo nearly joins, we are top in September then it all goes to pot

On the opening day of the 2002/03 season, I felt the fresh taste of hope in the air. The previous season had seen us spend most of the campaign in the top half of the league, competing for Europe and we had crushed our Chelsea hoodoo with an incredible 5-1 win against them in the Worthington Cup semi-final. Although we'd lost that final, somehow despite being the better team on the day, to Blackburn, our younger players who Hoddle had begun blooding in the side when he came in were starting to show bags of potential. We had Ledley at the back, a faster, more consistent upgrade on Judas, Simon "Digger" Davies tearing up and down the wing and after a season on the sidelines Stephen Carr was coming back and before injury, Christian Ziege had looked great on the other wing. My bias towards older players had been sorely tested too as Teddy Sheringham, who had returned from Man Utd on a two-year deal, Les Ferdinand and former Chelsea midfielder Gustavo Poyet had a hugely successful season in front of goal, with their combined 42 goals in all competitions betraying their combined 96 years of age! Club record signing Sergei Rebrov couldn't get a look in and with a 3-5-2 system employed by Hoddle, who had also splashed £8m on Southampton defender Dean Richards the previous season, this blend of youth and experience would surely drive us on in the coming months.

There were just two summer acquisitions, which I found disappointing after such an exciting World Cup in Japan and South Korea but we had been told that we had tried to go big. Remember Rivaldo? The Brazilian WC winner had dazzled at the tournament and played alongside Ronaldo (the original one, complete with a weird beaver haircut) and Ronaldinho had led his country to glory. Well, he was out of contract after the tournament after the 30-year-old chose not to extend his stay at Barcelona. The former Ballon d'Or recipient was being trailed heavily by Hoddle and new chairman Daniel Levy, who were licking their lips at the possibility of signing him.

Sadly though, Rivaldo plumped for Olympiakos, favouring the Greek outfit over a stay in N17, leading to much ridicule from rival fans and even media outlets like Sky Sports, after the Brazilian had written a letter of apology to the club and Levy issued a statement boasting about how we nearly signed one of the best players in the world but ultimately hadn't. I was crestfallen. I'd even signed him to Tottenham on FIFA!

Instead, Spurs plumped for two other midfielders in Rivaldo's absence. Jamie Redknapp, who was out of contract at Liverpool after missing lots of playing time due to injury, signed right at the end of the previous season. I was happy with him as coincidentally he was already in my FIFA team, but the reality of his signing was arguably as big a statement as to where Tottenham were at the time than Rivaldo's potential transfer.

We were still seen as mid-table no-hopers, who might do well in the cups but fail to upset the established order at the top of the table, so signing midfielders who barely had a better injury record than certain members of our squad, whilst adding strength in numbers didn't say much about how we could push on. Neither did the capture of Red Star Belgrade man Milenko Acimovic, who I got excited about as he scored for Slovenia at the World Cup but I was probably the only person in the fanbase feeling that way.

Why couldn't we sign anybody who could set the world on fire? Another Klinsmann would do so, but considering we had that in the unfair comparisons with the injury-prone Steffen Iversen, who else was there to act as our talisman, especially as Teddy was 37 and out of contract at the end of the season?

Thank god for Peter Ridsdale.

The Leeds chairman had overseen a moderate period in the Yorkshire club's success after spending big on names like Rio Ferdinand, Mark Viduka, Robbie Fowler and Seth Johnsen, the fairy tale was beginning to turn into a nightmare. The club failed to qualify for the Champions League and the revenue stream had dried up. There was a host of stars, mainly homegrown like Jonathan Woodgate, Alan Smith and Paul Robinson, all beginning to stake claims for international places, who were on big contracts and soon, Leeds United were hosting a fire sale. And they had just the person we were looking for marooned on the bench.

In 2002 Robbie Keane's stock was sky-high. He'd helped the Republic of Ireland reach the last 16 of the World Cup, scoring three goals at the tournament and at 22 years old, he was still thought of as one of the most exciting talents in the country. Sure, he'd been around a bit, having already turned out for Wolves, Coventry, Inter Milan and Leeds in a short career to date but he needed somewhere where his talents would shine and he could call home. Tottenham would be just that and in the first summer transfer window we stumped up a bargain £7m for Keano, just before it slammed shut and he was announced to the crowd just before our fourth game of the season, a 2-1 win over Southampton that saw us go top.

First. In the Premier League. I felt dizzy. I even got chills when I put the little cardboard Tottenham tab at the top of my Match magazine League table standings poster. We'd have injuries at the start of the season, didn't we always, but this time it wasn't affecting us. We'd won three and drawn one of our opening fixtures and now we sat top of the pile. I was made up. At the time my best friend was a gloating Gooner, who delighted in tormenting me when Judas left for his lot and they won their second double in four years. The joy and one-upmanship were short-lived sadly, but boy did I milk it!

Although we soon fell off the perch, we still stuck around the top places for a large majority of the season. After ten games, Keano had scored twice against Bolton Wanderers in a 3-1 win at the Lane that saw us sit first. For the umpteenth time in my supporting life, we'd drawn against the Scum at home, thanks to a Christian Ziege free-kick that is only marginally worse off than the Gazza one a decade earlier. We bettered Blackburn away, beat Leeds at home with Keano scoring a wonder strike and went away to Manchester City in their shiny new stadium and beat them 3-2 also. In fact, by the New Year, we were sitting in the top six.

Sadly, our cup runs were non-existent. We went out to Division One side Burnley in the fourth round of the League Cup and were humiliated on live tele when the BBC showed us getting thrashed 4-0 by finalists Southampton in the third round but I was still buoyant about our season. My Dad, less so. A seasoned campaigner, who had been hurt many times before, felt duty-bound to keep my expectations in check.

How right he was to do so. After Christmas, we only won 5 out of the remaining league games, including a memorable 4-3 thriller against Everton in which Robbie Keane scored his first hat-trick. In the end, with the final two games of the season being a total and utter shit show. First, we lost to Middlesborough 5-1 at the Riverside then, at the final game of the season in which we were saying our final goodbyes to Teddy Sheringham and Steffen Freund, we were humiliated 4-0 by Blackburn. By then I knew that things were going to end up the way they always did after a 2-0 defeat at home to Man City on Easter Monday. I was out playing football with my mates, as I did most days Spurs played back then, and when the results started coming through, my fellow 12-13-year-olds all laughed at me. I was around a friend of mine, who had just started taking a keen interest in Chelsea, watching Soccer Saturday as the Middlesborough goals were coming up on the vidprinter. I wanted to run and hide.

With 14 wins, 8 draws and 16 defeats we finished tenth, ten points from a UEFA Cup place and eight points above West Ham who astonishingly were relegated, despite their wealth of talent and having Les Ferdinand, who we'd offloaded to them in January. Sheringham bowed out with a joint top score of 13 goals along with his apprentice Robbie Keane and that was kind of it. I still wore my horrendously tight navy-blue Kappa shirt well into that summer with what little pride I could. After all, we nearly signed Rivaldo, you know!

So it was the same old, same old come the end of the season and Hoddle had to work his magic fast, not just to turn the club around but to stop the humiliation I was experiencing at school and at my local park!

The 2002-03 away kit, first bought for me when I was 13, modelled by me aged 30! Thank god for stretchy Kappa kits, 2019

2003/04 - Hoddle's not the messiah and that lot wins the league at the Lane and goes unbeaten

In a parallel world, this was the season an ultimately shady Russian billionaire called Roman Abramovich bought our club, turned us into title chasers and started a period of unbelievable success both domestically and on the continent. However, Abramovich's helicopter took a detour over West London and he cancelled his appointment with Daniel Levy and ENIC and purchased Chelsea instead.

For me, this is the worst season Tottenham Hotspur has played out in my lifetime. It was one full of terrible lows and well, that's probably as good as it got. After the dismal surrender to bad form last season Glenn Hoddle was under pressure to deliver, especially as once again Daniel Levy and ENIC had allowed him to spend what little money they were willing to give him on freshening up the club's attacking talent.

Out went old names and deadwood like Sheringham, Freund, Iversen, Rebrov, Sherwood, Perry, Thatcher and Sullivan and in came...well, nothing but strikers. Good ones at that, at least on paper. The marque signing was undoubtedly that of Portuguese forward Helder Postiga, for £6.25m from Josè Mourinho's Porto. The young striker had had an impressive season previously and Hoddle bought him to nurture his talent alongside two other recruits who were more familiar with English football. We plundered West Ham, who were now in Division One, now called the Championship, for the signature of Frederic Kanoute.

The French forward joined us for £3.5m and looked like the obvious choice to partner Robbie Keane up front but Hoddle wasn't done yet. He also signed the highly-rated Brighton man Bobby Zamora, at a snip for £1.5m.

But for a team that lacked solidity at the back, where were the defensive recruits, I hear you ask? Well, we picked up some bloke called Mbulelo Mabizela from Orlando Pirates after we played them on a South African trip, yes, that was it. In a back four that saw the names of Gary "the Ginger Pele" Doherty, Goran Bunjevcevic, who we signed back in 2001 but who was so absent from our side that my uncle didn't know who he was until he turned on a FIFA game he played with me, and Anthony Gardner, confidence wasn't high going into the new season. Kasey Keller had made the number one spot his own and Stephen Carr, who despite being made captain whenever Jamie Redknapp was missing (which was a lot) and was looking more and more annoyed that he was still playing for us, and Mauricio Taricco was vying with a now injury-riddled Christian Ziege for the left side of the defence. We were screwed. Even the signing of Paul Konchesky on loan did little to excite although Stefan Dalmat, the tricky French winger on loan from Inter Milan, looked tasty but we looked rubbish from the outset.

I knew it, you knew it. When we went into our opening day defeat away to Birmingham, it already looked like Hoddle was on borrowed time.

Sure, we still had Ledley, but the King of the Lane had already endured time out on the sidelines this early into his career so we had to make do with what we could most weeks and by the time we faced Southampton, six games and one victory into the new season the final whistle was blown on Glenn's time as Spurs manager. The man who returned to White Hart Lane as our messiah had failed. He'd taken us to one League Cup final, which we conspired to lose, and that was about it in his two-and-a-half years as our manager. Levy needed to act and quickly. The team were in for a relegation scrap and we were managerless. I was also terrified that Robbie Keane would leave as soon as he could. I did wonder who would jump ship when the transfer window reopened.

With no immediate successor to be found, Levy appointed former manager and then Director of Football David Pleat as caretaker until the end of the season. There was a slight manager bounce including a 0-0 draw away to Man City (in which we didn't register a shot on goal), a 3-0 hammering of Everton at home (including a brilliant long-range thunder bastard from Freddie Kanoute) and the 2-1 win at struggling Leicester, where Mabizela introduced himself to many a pub quiz in the land with a gorgeous strike from the edge of the box.

But after that, form began to tank again and so did the results, culminating in a depressing week in which we went out of the League Cup on penalties to eventual winners Middlesborough at the quarter-finals stage and got humiliated at St James Park again. Laurent Robert scored two goals of the season contenders in the 4-0 rout but that did little to comfort us and we went into 2004 staring down the barrel. I was having flashbacks to that winter of 1997 when all seemed lost. Kanoute even changed his nationality to Malian and was going to represent his new motherland in the African Cup of Nations in January, surely in a ploy to get away from N17 for a bit. What Spurs needed was a new face to come in and boost the club.

Step forward Jermain Defoe. The young talented striker had caused a stir at West Ham for handing in his transfer request the very same afternoon they were relegated from the Premiership. He had also, despite scoring frequently in the Championship, been sent off for the Hammers a few times. Despite the disciplinary record, Defoe was a frustrated figure and wanted out. Pleat was only too happy to oblige and at £7m he joined. We even managed to flog new boy Booby Zamora the other way, who had failed to adapt to the rigours of the top flight and only scored one goal for the club, ironically, in a 1-0 win over West Ham in that season's Carling Cup.

By the time that Defoe made his debut, we'd endured a festive period where we had lost four games in a row and Postiga, who played 24 games that season, had only scored twice. We had also just suffered the pain of a second humiliating comeback in the space of a few seasons.

In an FA Cup fourth-round replay we soared into a 3-0 lead at half-time thanks to goals from Ledley King (who we no longer had at the back because Pleat was playing him in midfield alongside January signing Michael Brown), Robbie Keane and Christian Ziege. We were flying and City had Joey Barton sent off in the tunnel at half-time. Surely, we would cruise into the fifth round now against a side with ten men?

What followed was so gut-wrenchingly humiliating it made one boy at school go up to his Dad and tell him that he didn't want to be a Spurs fan anymore. We all had PTSD from the United game in 2001 which ended 5-3 after being 3-0 up at the break and when City drew level through Shaun Wright-Phillips, I stared at my radio, the one I had spent years tuning so I could alternate between Radio Five Live and Radio London. I felt like crying. Surely not again, surely!?

Before you could say who the **** is Jonathan Macken, Jonathan Macken rose highest to a cross and sent the ball flying past the despairing Kasey Keller to score a late winner, cement a 4-3 comeback, dump us out of the cup and condemn Spurs to being the laughing stock of the footballing world again. I knew what was coming the following day at school. The ridicule, the smug grins, the pointing, the laughing. I got so cross thinking about it that I yanked the radio from the plug and threw it at the wardrobe. In the dark of the night, I could see glints of what used to be its white plastic casing shatter on impact. I heard the unmistakable sound of my Father rushing up the stairs to see what the commotion was (my sisters were eleven and four respectively at this point) about to bollock his fourteen-year-old son for potentially waking the house up. When he saw the look on my face and the radio smashed on the floor, he realised what had happened.

"They didn't, did they?" he asked.

I nodded solemnly.

He shook his head and closed the door, nothing else was said. It was probably the lowest I had felt as a fan up to that point.

Thankfully, with a young dynamic strike partnership in the guise of Keano and JD, we started to score by the bucketful. Four against Portsmouth, four against Charlton and four against Leicester in a 4-4 draw that was both bat shit crazy and the Ginger Pele's worst 90 minutes in a Tottenham shirt. It was clear Spurs had some players they could build around for the future.

There were just two small problems. One – we still had a quarter of the season to play out with the garbage we had in the current squad and we didn't want to flirt anymore with relegation. On that front, luckily, Leicester, Leeds and Wolves were truly atrocious that season and all finished on 33 points and we settled on 45, with 19 games lost – a record in the 20-team season for us. We only won 13 with a goal difference of minus 10 having conceded 57 compared to 47 scored. We were shit and we knew it and the second problem? Well, that lot down the road was about to embarrass us all over again.

It was a horrific time to have a best friend as a Gooner. Not only in our teenage friendship had I endured them winning the double and then the FA Cup a year later, I'd watched our treacherous captain run down his contract and join them for nothing and now, NAME REDACTED had played an integral part in that lot going for an entire season unbeaten. What was worse, if they escaped defeat in our clash on the 25th of April, they would win the league at White Hart Lane, for the second time in their history.

Mathematically this wasn't the nail-biting affair where we needed something from it to stay up but if we obtained a point from this game there was no way we'd go down. How far we had fallen that I was willing, as I sat pressed against my parents' radio (I'd been made to promise I wouldn't break this one if we lost) to celebrate like we'd won the league ourselves after. It had been that kind of a season. We hadn't won since the 3rd March, indeed, we'd only win another two games this season anyway, so I needed something, anything to hang onto as I knew that anything less than a victory for Spurs meant full bragging rights for the rest of time from my friend. Again, I'm thankful that this was in an age before social media, when the Gooner family at the bottom of my road and my friend were the worst I had to deal with. I'd hate to see the Samaritan's switchboard if this season were to play out in the Twitter/X age!

My head was in my hands as I heard the Scum go 2-0 up in the first half. I kept my Dad, who was gardening, abreast of the updates by shouting out of the window into our garden. I punched the air when Jamie Redknapp got one back and prayed we'd find another couple more. We were playing for pride and despite being outplayed in the first half, had shown grit and application in the second half. Then, right before the end, Gooners keeper Jens Lehmann and Robbie Keane got in a scrap, resulting in a yellow card for both but more importantly a penalty to Spurs! Keano slotted it home, ensuring we'd be a Premier League side the following season but also at the final whistle, the

Scum had done it and now I don't want to type anymore about it.

So, you see, sometimes the very definition of a terrible season is entwined with the success of your rivals. I'd had enough. We'd been managerless since September, and despite the likes of King, Keane and Defoe proving their worth, I had begun to dislike the team. The players who had once adorned my wall were being taken down and replaced with bands such as Oasis, The Strokes and Syd Barrett. When 14th place was confirmed and the season was over, club servants such as Darren Anderton were unceremoniously released. Gus Poyet and Christian Ziege were also let go. Postiga returned to Porto, who had won the treble, including the Champions League in his absence, and within six months Doherty, Redknapp, Mabizela, Taricco and Keller had all been offloaded also.

Levy decided it was time to build a continental approach to running the club, with Frank Arnesen as sporting director, Martin Jol as first team coach and France manager Jacques Santini appointed as manager after a long and sometimes desperate appointment process.

I was actually in Disneyland Paris with my family when it was announced Santini would join us after the European Championships that summer. It was a day when I was spoken to in very angry ways by some of the native people in the capital, picking me out for wearing my navy blue 2002/03 shirt. I just thought, like everyone else except us Spurs fans, that we were hated in France. It wasn't until we went back to our hotel that I read the news and decided against wearing another Spurs shirt on the holiday.

By the time Spurs returned to Premier League action in August, the side was almost unrecognisable. Barring King, Davies, Defoe, Kanoute and Keane, the entire squad had been overhauled. Club favourite Stephen Carr had even left for Newcastle which was a huge blow but I thought understandable for a man who had such promise as a youngster but who had been tarred and feathered by such a poor side at the time.

At least he didn't join that lot down the road...

2007/08 - Yes, we won the League Cup but...

This was a tricky one to include on this list. Yes, we won the League Cup in a glorious victory over Chelsea but this was also the season that we started the season as potential title challengers, had a manager sacked during a game, the players lost the ketchup in the club canteen and our two best players left at the end. It was a rollercoaster alright and for this eighteen-year-old it was a bitch of a kind of year that I had too!

There was so much to look forward to. Under the popular Martin Jol, we'd come on in leaps and bounds since our days as Premier League nomads. We'd finished fifth two seasons in a row, having not reached those lofty heights for 15 years previously and in a team that boasted young, homegrown talent like England's number 1 Paul Robinson, Aaron Lennon, Tom Huddlestone, Ledley King, Michael Dawson, Jermaine Jenas and Jermain Defoe, mixed with arguably the best striking partnership in my lifetime in

Dimitar Berbatov and Robbie Keane, there was lots to look forward to going into our 125th anniversary season.

To help bolster our squad, Jol went big on England striker Darren Bent. At £16.5m from Charlton, the prolific forward came in with over 30 goals in the last two seasons in the league and bolstered an already frightening attack. We also spent £8m on centre-back Younes Kaboul from Auxerre and £5m on some teenager from the Championship called Gareth Bale, who I knew nothing about, only that he was a month younger than me and so it dawned on me, despite only ever playing park and school football, that I'd never make it in the Prem. He was highly thought of in the footballing world and could take a mean free-kick, and we'd beaten Man Utd to his signature, so despite knowing very little about Bale, I was hyped he had joined us. We also brought in Kevin-Prince Boateng from Hertha Berlin and another teenager by the name of Danny Rose on a free from Leeds.

The squad was dripping with talent, all the paper talk was that with these new acquisitions, we were going for the title and Jol was the man who would bring us the glory we craved.

So how come we only won one game in the league between August and November? And that was to Derby, who set the record for the lowest points tally in Premier League history this season! Christ, I had two relationships crash and burn in between those two wins. What was happening? This was supposed to be our year.

In truth, Jol looked broken. There was lots of talk regarding his future at the club. Levy had already been papped courting Sevilla manager Juande Ramos and Jol's frustration at not being allowed to bring in Martin Petrov or Stuart Downing as his new left winger in the summer had also been well documented. With the talent we had at our disposal, it was unfathomable that we were so crap.

However, on the pitch, some of our key members were suffering. Paul Robinson had been the victim of a hideous bobbled back pass from Gary Neville in a crucial Euro 2008 qualifier which crushed the keeper's confidence. Michael Dawson was struggling without his defensive partner Ledley King, who by this point was missing more game time than he was playing, so despite us scoring we were shipping goals by the plentiful. Injuries reared their ugly head again and on the opening day a team fielding a back four of Pascal Chimbonda, Kaboul, Anthony Gardner and Paul Stalteri filling in on the left for the injured Lee-Young Pyo, went down to a last-minute winner away to Sunderland.

Indeed, the previous season, despite our 5th place finish, we only kept six clean sheets. It was clear something needed to be done. There were some very entertaining, yet very frustrating draws in that period. I'm playing them down. They were mental.

Firstly, we squandered a 3-1 lead away to Fulham to share the points 3-3, then in our 125th birthday match at home to Aston Villa, a crowd featuring such legends as Dave Mackay, Cliff Jones, Stevie Perryman and David Ginola watched as we fell behind 4-1. Trust

Spurs to not even get their birthday game right. I didn't watch it. I was out playing five-a-side football that night but I did see that Craig Gardner had put the Villan's fourth goal in on Teletext before I left with the hump. Then we got a goal back through Chimbonda, of all people. Then Keane scored a penalty ten minutes from time, leaving Younes Kaboul to level with a thunderbolt in the 94th minute, leading to a bundle of players and management staff on the bench and a home faithful going berserk. I wish I'd gone down to the pub to watch it.

I did catch up on the highlights later that night when somebody put up some blurry footage from Setanta Sports live coverage on this awesome new website called YouTube. It left me feeling positive that a week later we'd get something up at Anfield, going to show how fickle I was as a fan that a barely functioning side could go to a place we hadn't won at in nearly 15 years and take all three points and yet we nearly did! A Robbie Keane double, clearly auditioning for a move to his "boyhood club" the following season, put us 2-1 up only for us to casually concede a late equaliser to Fernando Torres.

Following another defeat away to Newcastle, we were 18th in the table but we had the distraction of a UEFA Cup group stage tie with Getafe at the Lane in midweek. I travelled to the Midlands, clutching every straw I could find that I'd be able to patch up my relationship with my ex-girlfriend, who had dumped me for University that summer. Christ, and I thought Judas moving to Arsenal was painful.

Every Spurs fan probably remembers where they were when they heard the news that Martin Jol had been sacked mid-game. I was in the bath! My bandmate Chris called me from home to tell me the news and then I hung up on him as my Dad was calling me too. I nearly dropped the phone in the water. I felt sick. All I could think about was how sorry I felt for Martin. Sure, he had no hair but we didn't care. The man loved us and we loved him back. He'd given us hope again and now Daniel Levy, Dr Evil as I started calling him at this point, loomed high above him in the director's box surely bricking it when the news leaked around the ground and Jol's name was sung loud and proud, even whilst losing yet again to the Spanish minnows.

It was a disgraceful way to dismiss someone who had done so much in restoring Tottenham's pride inside and outside of the club and Levy – who was already obsessing over plans for a new stadium – really should have hung his head in shame. Still, it was blindingly obvious who was to come in and Ramos was our man, after watching us from the stands lose once again to Blackburn, that is. The Spaniard, who had won the UEFA Cup with Sevilla in the previous two seasons, instrumented a new fitness regime for the squad and set about banning certain condiments from the canteen in Spurs Lodge. Ketchup was out of the window and for a while Spurs looked leaner and stronger as a unit, winning 5 games over December, including a 5-1 drubbing of Fulham on Boxing Day followed three days later by an incredible 6-4 win over Reading. Berbatov helped himself to four very well-taken goals in a match that had me hopping all over the living room watching Soccer Saturday on a rare weekend off.

The trouble around this point was that I wasn't able to go to any matches as I was working my first Saturday job in a shop and also couldn't drive, so unless I went with my parents to our annual pre-season home-friendly, this was a lean period for me. I did manage to sneak many lunchtime games by watching the screen from the Cross Keys Hotel in Saffron Walden, which was one road across from my work (I distinctly remember watching Berbatov's brilliant finish against the Scum in a 2-1 defeat at the Emirates this way). Another good spell of league form in the New Year meant we were pretty much safe from any threat of going down but it was all about the cups from here on in. After our glorious Carling Cup final victory against huge favourites Chelsea saw us qualify for Europe again the following year, our form became more patchy again in the league, only winning three of the final 12 games. A disappointing penalty shoot-out exit against a Hereleo Gomes-inspired PSV saw us crash out of Europe in the last 16, leading to two months of mad results (4-0 win over West Ham, a 4-4 draw with Chelsea and a 4-1 defeat away to Birmingham City) as we finished up a very comfortable 11th on 46 points, winning only 11 games but scoring 66 goals with 61 against us (we also scored 100 goals in all competitions for the second season in a row).

So, although we won a trophy, 2007-08 may have been entertaining and successful in one way, but in another we had gone spectacularly backwards in the league. With Ramos recruiting defenders such as Jonathan Woodgate, Alan Hutton and Gilberto in January it was clear the squad needed some work. There was a massive turnover of players in the summer of 2008 and trouble was on the horizon yet again. The Carling Cup victory was undoubtedly the high point of the team that had been built by Jol over the last few years but Ramos was about to rip it up and start again...

2013/14 - Bale-less Spurs, the magnificent seven, thrashings galore and Tim Sherwood and his gilet

Ah, I remember this one fondly. I was reporting on my beloved club almost every week for Goal at this point, in the capacity as a newswriter and as a Live Text Commentator so I was having a really fun time...typing from home on my bed watching dodgy feeds because they didn't pay the majority of their staff a living wage. Still, when it went tits up this season, at least I wasn't there squirming in person.

I feel that I should caveat at this point that you'll start to see a stark difference in what qualifies as a bad season for Tottenham. Whereas in the past sections, you'll have noticed that we were dicing with danger at the foot of the table or suffering boring, monotonous dreary football that led to nowt, in the 2010s things changed for us to such a degree that a bad season is one in which we didn't finish in the top 4. Such was our progression up until this point it does have to be commended how our failures from hereon in would be regarded as huge successes for most clubs in England. You're probably reading this thinking, "how the eff can a season in which we won 21 league games, had a 100% record in the Europa League group stage and between them, our keepers made 21 clean sheets be a disaster?" Indeed, show a Spurs fan from the 1993-94 or 1997-98 era of our beloved club this season and their heart would stop in shock and surprise. If nothing else, it makes my writing of these last four seasons in our bottom eleven a little more enjoyable!

That doesn't mean, however, that the embarrassment of being a Spurs fan would let up in places and nothing epitomises the hide-behind-the-corner flag moments of shame more than 2013/14.

That summer seemed all about one thing: was Gareth Bale staying or was he going? Our Welsh wizard had won the Footballer of the Year award and had almost single-handedly taken us into the top 4 – if it were not for the Scum pipping us by one point for the second consecutive season. His wonder goals and man-of-the-match performances had every media outlet under the sun talking up a huge move abroad, no more than the Spanish magazine Marca. At the time we had a youngster in the reserves called Kenny McEvoy who was the spitting image of Bale and I was begging Levy to dupe Real Madrid with him instead! Sadly, however, it looked like Bale would indeed be on his way out the door to join up with Luka Modrić and his fellow galacticos. The biggest indicator? Daniel Levy was splashing the cash...

We broke our transfer record thrice that summer, first with midfielder Paulinho joining from Corinthians for

£17m. Forward Nacer Chadli moved to N17 next for £7m from Twente, then Roberto Soldado, one of La Liga's most impressive strikers of recent seasons was recruited for a record £26m and Etienne Capoue completed the quartet before opening day for £9m. Soldado got off the mark with a penalty in a 1-0 win at Crystal Palace and at our first home game I watched him slot another one in against Swansea as we won again!

But there was still more to come. Vlad Chiriches, Christian Eriksen and record £30m signing Erik Lamela arrived just before the window shut. Levy had spent £109m in one summer and pundits were starting to see us as proper title contenders, even without Bale. On 1st September 2013, a move announced at the end of the window, Gareth had joined Real Madrid for a world record £85.5m. We hid our disappointment with our seven shiny new signings and early season form. Even Garth Crooks uttered the line, "Spurs have sold Elvis and bought The Beatles!" The Magnificent Seven had an awful lot of hype to live up to...

By December, despite an impressive run in Europe, Spurs and AVB had suffered several humiliating defeats domestically, an early season one to the Scum, where we looked blunter than a pair of safety scissors, a disastrous 3-0 defeat at home to West Ham (they did the treble over us this season, but didn't like to mention it at the time...) a game in which Tim Krul's record-breaking 14 saves meant we went down 1-0 to Newcastle then we lost 6-0 to Man City, with Jesus Navas starting the rout in the first minute! After a couple of tight squeaks past Fulham and Sunderland,

AVB was fast running out of time. Still smarting from the club's inability to get João Moutinho over the line on deadline day, Willian's disrespectful medical with us then buggering off to Chelsea, and having fallen out with the press and the fans after he criticised their reaction to quite turgid performances, the Portuguese manager needed a result against high-flying Liverpool.

They destroyed us. A terrible 5-0 loss in the rain at the Lane meant it was the end of AVB. The club was now languishing in 7th and were a long, long away from the pack at the top, with Liverpool especially really starting to look like title contenders, Spurs had been beaten by all their closest title rivals and for fans and a chairman who wanted more, it just wasn't good enough. Former player now coach Tim Sherwood was promoted and simultaneously uncomplicated our tactics and brought players like Emanuel Adebayor in from the cold and was paid immediately with a six-game unbeaten run into the new year to get the club back into European contention.

But our biggest failing that season was our inability to overcome the bigger hurdles in front of us. We were thrashed at home again 5-1 by Man City, who by now were starting their catch-up with runaway leaders Liverpool and with so many new players and outgoings (fan favourite Jermain Defoe left for Toronto in Canada in January) we looked disjointed and like a team well and truly in transition. Plus, our acquisitions in the summer by and large weren't working out. Soldado was struggling to settle and no matter how hard we willed him to be successful

Adebayor was the better striker for us that season. There was even a youngster named Harry Kane who started popping up with a goal or two later on in the season but it was clear that Sherwood was a little out of his depth. Only Christian Eriksen and arguably Nacer Chadli, who had been the cheapest of the summer signings were producing the goods. Even old heads like Michael Dawson and Aaron Lennon were starting to look like their best days were behind them and we missed the likes of Bale, Modrić, King and Van der Vaart, who had all left in the twelve months previously. Our spine just wasn't strong enough yet. We had Lloris, Vertonghen, Dembele and Kane, yes, but their time in a much better side was yet to come. For now, Spurs looked just what they were. The best of the rest.

Sure, we could beat pretty much everyone below us (except bloody West Ham, it seemed) but all of those above us ground us into the dirt with every game. Chelsea did us over 4-0 and then the scoreline was repeated at Anfield, where Jan Vertonghen looked disinterested in the tunnel before the game, the players by and large looked unhappy and unmotivated and our fans were even singing, "Let's pretend we scored a goal!" followed by a massive ironic cheer. Gallows humour if ever there was any.

There were a few highlights, of course. An impressive 3-2 comeback against Mauricio Pochettino's Southampton, a 5-1 hammering of Sunderland, including a first Premier League goal for Kane and a second consecutive victory over Manchester United at Old Trafford to name a few. By

May, Sherwood, who had been given an 18-month contract, didn't look like he'd last past the final day of the campaign and despite playing younger players like Danny Rose, Nabil Bentaleb and Harry Kane more regularly than his predecessors, and boasting about his win percentage, time was up and Spurs were looking for yet another dream.

2019/20 - Poch is sacked for Mourinho, Amazon films our post-CL implosion and there's a global pandemic

There's a Blur song on their self-titled 1997 album that I think fits this season perfectly. Death of a Party. It was the end, rightly or wrongly, of Mauricio Pochettino's magical time in charge of us, being given his marching orders just five months after he nearly took us to the brink of football nirvana. Looking back now we were all putting on a brave face after the Champions League final defeat to Liverpool. We got ourselves hyped for our first full season in our brand spanking shiny new stadium, splashed the cash in the transfer market for the first time in 18 months on Tanguy Ndombele for £55m, our new club record, Giovanni Lo Celso and Ryan Sessegnon, who both came in from PSG and Fulham and suddenly we'd spent £120m on new faces – something big clubs like us could now do with the stadium and regular Champions League football.

But that final broke Poch and it broke some of the players too. By November we had only won 3 of our first 12 games and been hopelessly taken apart by

Bayern Munich when former Gooner Serge Gnabry put four past Hugo Lloris to thrash us 7-2 at our new home. The spark was gone and Daniel Levy knew it. With Amazon cameras following every little detail of what was going on, he needed a star to put at the front of his new show and found it in former Chelsea and Manchester United boss Josè Mourinho.

Josè seemed like the right appointment for a team who were going places. He had won more cups than we had as a club (something he was soon boasting about to the media), had a winning mentality, was a tactical genius (a-ba-bee-a-ba-ba!) and according to Levy, was one of two of the best managers on the planet and he knew how to get the best out of our players. He knew how to coach world-class players and we had Kane, Son and Dele, three of the best in the league. Then again, Jan Vertonghen and Toby Alderweireld were beginning to show their age and were running their contracts down as was Christian Eriksen who wanted a move away. Josè was a master at bigging up players who were potentially running low on confidence (telling Davinson Sanchez that when his United side faced Ajax in the Europa League final that he looked shit scared) and finally, he looked like a man who could bring us the thing that we were craving. Silverware.

Mourinho won wherever he went and yes, it all inevitably crashed and burnt with him in the end but Spurs fans by and large were willing to sacrifice their swashbuckling brand of attacking football for a more pragmatic approach IF it was to lead to glory.

This season we were having to rely on many things, one such factor being that of an impending European ban for Man City which meant that Spurs would qualify again for the Champions League so long as they finished fifth. That never came to fruition, surprisingly as the ban was overturned. Fifth would be the highest we'd get that season under Mourinho as injuries to key players (Lloris pretty much snapped his elbow in a 3-0 defeat at Brighton, Kane tore his hamstring on New Year's Day and Son broke his arm early on in a 3-2 win at Villa but was then told he would have to have it operated on and would miss the season) meant that in Josè's words we were "****ed".

Only rare highlights such as the 5-0 win over Burnley in December, complete with Puskás award-winning goal from Son (I was on my honeymoon in Mexico, watching the game on my phone from my deck chair), and a 2-0 win over Josè's old foe Pep Guardiola and Man City thanks to goals from debutant Steven Bergwijn and Son but in truth, the club was brought to its knees by the injuries to key players.

With an injury-ravaged squad limping out of the FA Cup on penalties to Norwich in a game which saw an infamous moment where Eric Dier stomped his way into the crowd to have it out with a fan, and a lacklustre two-legged performance in the last 16 of the CL against Leibzig, the season was pretty much done in March.

Worse was to come. In the early days of 2020, COVID-19 started to make its way around the world, taking the lives of millions of people and life as we knew it, and football, was locked down.

A global pandemic didn't stop Josè Mourinho trying to get the best out of Tanguy, though, as he comically made the underperforming Frenchman train in a local park. When football and the country started unlocking a bit in the summer, Spurs, with eight games to go, were one of the sides who looked like they would benefit greatly from the enforced break. Son and Kane were back and even if there was nobody there to watch at the grounds, at least football was back.

Our only defeat in this period came away to bogey team Sheffield United when we met again with a new worst enemy. VAR. In the build-up to a Kane goal, Lucas Moura had been flattened and the ball was kicked against his arm by a United player and subsequently, VAR disallowed it. We went on to lose 3-1 and bemoan yet another dodgy decision (it had also chalked off a Serge Aurier goal away to Leicester for an incorrect offside which, quite possibly, might have seen us win and Poch keep his job).

Watching every game from my living room, I loved having football and Spurs back in my life, especially when Alderwiereld rose highest in our 2-1 win against the Gooners, who by now were hysterical mid-table no-hopers with a YouTube channel that had football fans of all clubs regularly crying with laughter, but it wasn't the same without the fans and fanless stadiums, like Josè's tactics, as something I was just going to have to put up with for now.

With a final game draw away to Crystal Palace, we secured a 6th place finish and Mourinho and his coaching staff celebrated like we won a cup. Sure, we'd qualified for the Europa League, but it was a bit embarrassing seeing people on social media saying that we'd brought Josè down to our level. In truth though, this stop/start topsy turvy season had been a disappointing one but surely, even in a world where COVID was still running rife, the good times are about to come back to Spurs?

2020-21 – Top in December, seventh in May, Josè sacked before final and Kane wants to leave as we join the European Super League

With us still not being allowed in the stadiums, we needed something to cheer us up following our 6th-place finish the previous campaign. Say what you like about Daniel Levy getting involved too much on the football front but in the Summer of 2020, it looked as though he had given Josè Mourinho a free reign to buy and sell whoever he wanted. With Harry Kane nearing 200 goals for his club and his partner Heung-Min Son nearing a century, we needed recruits to help push the side, and our current-day legends, over the finish line to glory.

First through the door was Pierre-Emile Hojbjerg in a money-plus swap deal with Southampton that saw Kyle Walker-Peters go the other way. The defensive midfielder, a self-proclaimed "Viking" was a player in the Josè mould and he soon added right-wing-back Matt Doherty from Wolves to compete with the inconsistent Serge Aurier for a starting place. He acquired cover in the form of former England keeper Joe Hart, striker Carlos Vinicius from Benfica as a backup for Kane, handy for the early stages of our

Europa League campaign, and then a double swoop from Real Madrid that had Spurs fans checking the sky trackers. Yes, Bale was back. Having won every trophy he could in Spain – including four Champions Leagues – our Welsh wizard was back. Older, wiser, and with the type of top knot that only a gammon can hate. He came back on a season-long loan accompanied by Spanish left-back Sergio Regulion, and Spurs fans were delirious with optimism. This side, in a first full season under Josè, with a forward line of Kane, Son and Bale? I was salivating.

After a dismal opening day defeat to Everton, we embarked on a run that saw Josè throw the shackles off his players and Tanguy Ndombele quite literally turned our season around with the kind of outrageous piece of skill we knew he had in his locker, as he put through to Kane who teed up Son for his first goal away to Southampton to equalise before half-time. Indeed, Son didn't stop there, with Kane laying four on for him and then helping himself to a goal to see us win 5-2. We would have felt hard done by if a VAR decision to rule a handball conceded by Matt Doherty had a bearing on the result but it was a bit of a warning that the new standard of officiating was still looking to balls up every club's afternoons.

Son looked delighted with his four goals until Josè interrupted his post-match MOTM presentation to tell him that Harry Kane was better on the day in a sort of weird sociopathic moment that would have made Brian Clough blush.

We were deprived of all three points against Newcastle when VAR gave a handball against Eric

Dier in the final minute of added-on time. The England international was facing the other way when Andy Carroll headed the ball down onto his outstretched arm and so most of football united in disgust at how ridiculous a decision it was, costing us two points that would bite us on the arse in May.

But the next two games were enthralling, mad and memorable for good and bad reasons. Firstly, we thrashed Man Utd 6-1 at Old Trafford, putting pay to years of the whole "lads, it's Tottenham" jibe from the Reds fans and condemning Ole Gunnar Solskjaer's team to their heaviest defeat at home to us in their history. We then went 3-0 up in no time at all at home to West Ham, and a new style of pragmatic yet gung-ho football was very unlike anything we'd seen from a Josè Mourinho side before and yet here it was, free-flowing and solid at the back. Until it wasn't. In the final ten minutes, the Hammers nicked a point, with Bale, making his first appearance back in our colours, missing an easy chance to put us 4-2 up. Manuel Lanzini's rocket following a tame Harry Winks clearance gave the Happy Hammers reasons to be cheerful, and Josè the excuse to go back to his attritional style of defensive, counter-attacking football.

Now that Mourinho had resorted back to type, the football became quite dull. We were willing to sacrifice style over results though, especially beating Man City, who by now despite their untold riches and trophy-laden squad still couldn't buy a win, or a goal, against us at the Tottenham Hotspur Stadium. Then the cherry on the top was the 2-0 demolition of Arsenal, a game in which some lucky fans got to witness a brilliant Son effort and a goal which made Harry Kane the most prolific player in North London derbies and we got to go top of the table, with the Scum dwindling in 12th. We were unbeaten in the league for three months until a tetchy unlucky late winner from Liverpool at our place knocked the stuffing out of the side. None more so than Steven Bergwijn. The Dutch winger missed two guilt-edge chances in the game, hitting the post when put through one-on-one with keeper Alisson, and was barely seen after that. Gareth Bale was not starting in the league either as Josè seemed to be making a point to his club, and his chairman in particular, that while he was around, nobody was bigger than him. It also brought into question whether Bale's return was a Daniel Levy signing as the coach began to drive a distance between himself and the players.

Despite our league form starting to slip, we were still going strong in the cups, something that was Mourinho's forte. We made it to the last 16 against Dinamo Zagreb and took a 2-0 scoreline into the second leg in Croatia. Our path into the quarter-finals was made all the easier as their manager at the time had just been sent to prison for tax fraud so surely we would sail through?

Nope. Mourinho set us up to defend what we had and Zagreb thrashed us 3-0. After the match, club captain Hugo Lloris came out and labelled our team a disgrace. Mourinho apologised to the fans and a trophy that we were in strong contention of winning had slipped through our grasp and we were the laughing stock of the footballing world once again.

We still had a chance of glory in the League Cup as we'd successfully negotiated our way to a final against Manchester City, beating Chelsea on penalties in an earlier round. However, Levy pulled the trigger on Mourinho just six days before the final. A lot of us fans were conflicted. Sure, we were fed up with Josè's tactics and the way he threw players under the bus whenever something didn't go our way but to dismiss a manager who was a specialist in big games seemed strange. But Levy felt compelled that the timing was right, possibly to cover up some impending news which was to shake European football, but also, as The Athletic stated in an article in April 2021, because:

"Tottenham players were left bored and untested by his training sessions.

Most of the squad was expecting his sacking.

Tactics were so obsessed with stopping opposition that players were unsure how to attack.

Mourinho's assistant Joao Sacramento was unpopular with the squad.

The club were unhappy with Mourinho's criticism of the players and asked him to stop it.

Mourinho ran out of allies at the club, on and off the pitch.

Only Harry Kane was loyal to Mourinho at the end.

His dismissal had nothing to do with the Super League and was based purely on results."

The installation of former player turned coach Ryan Mason, who was younger than several of Josè's ageing squad, also seemed to be a naive move.

Who knows if we would ever have got the trophy monkey off our back if Josè had been there on that sunny Wembley day in April but as it was, Pep's City triumphed over us with a late goal after we had played with our backs to the wall for most of the game. The familiar fog of depression enveloped me as I watched Fernandinho lift the League Cup instead of our own Hugo.

We had some fun games in the league, and indeed under both Mourinho and Mason we amassed 121 goals in all competitions, betraying our sluggish defensive style, but come our final home game of the season and a pathetic 2-1 defeat to Aston Villa, the rumour mill was up and running again as a visibly upset Harry Kane looked set to be on his way out the club who had failed to win any major honours or qualify for the Champions League, for the second successive season. The golden boot and golden assist winner had another brilliant year and was closing in on a seemingly impossible feat in overtaking Jimmy Greaves as our all-time club record goal scorer, but he was cutting a disconsolate shadow in N17.

Gary Neville and Sky Sports had done their best to stoke the fires in a hateful interview with Harry around a golf course in which he hinted explicitly that he might need to leave to get what he wanted and all of this was starting to happen at a time when the club announced that it was joining a breakaway European Super League, which sent a shockwave through the footballing world.

Why Spurs were included in the list of the European elite was a figure of bemusement and piss-taking for many in the media and on social outlets, but Levy had wanted Spurs involved so they could stay in touch with the mighty clubs he wanted us to become.

But the ESL would have destroyed the football pyramid and been a competition that was almost a closed shop, making the clubs involved richer and richer with no qualification or relegation to worry about.

It was a total scandal and added to the list of terrible things that Daniel Levy had wanted to do with Tottenham up to this point.

As the backlash was felt all across Europe the clubs that had signed up to the proposal started to pull out one-by-one, each issuing an apology.

Not Tottenham though.

We stayed in until the very last moment and issued a pitiful, "Sorry this decision upset you", nonsense statement.

With the club's best player wanting out, another false dawn coming to a close and more wrong decisions than a man driving a golf buggy naked the wrong way down the M25, Levy knew that his next move had to be the right one to get everyone back on side...

Sophie and I at a friendly between Cambridge United and Tottenham

My Mum with William in the manager's seat, Tottenham Hotspur Stadium tour, 2021

2022-23 – Conte stricken, our coach passes away, everything burns and Levy feels the heat

As I write this, I'm still pissed off with these last two entries. Steam is pouring out of my ears and my eyes are bulging as I type through gritted fingers. How could we have got it so wrong? We reached the Champions League final, for crying out loud, and for four years after it was by and large rubbish. I'll barely be writing about the football on the pitch, I feel as it was so full of incidents! Ugh, okay, last season now...

Things were looking rosy again as we went into the 2022-23 season. Another former Chelsea man in the form of Antonio Conte had come in and again, the football was turgid and counter-attack based. We still had too many players from the Poch era hanging around and starting for us with club captain Hugo Lloris looking past it, Eric Dier, Ben Davies and Davinson Sanchez, who despite also being loyal club servants were originally backup for superior players Jan Vertonghen, Toby Alderwiereld and Danny Rose a few years back and expensive club signings Tanguy Ndombele and Giovanni Lo Celso were so far removed from the squad that they had been banished on loan.

But Levy had attempted to listen to the disgruntled supporters and removed himself from the footballing side of things to run booking more corporate events at the Tottenham Hotspur Stadium and keeping the riches flooding in. In his place stood Managing Director Fabio Paratici, who despite an investigation lingering over his time at Juventus, actually looked like he was doing a decent job in finding talent around Europe. Our recruitment policy had improved since the days of Steve "I hate the January transfer window" Hitchin, and thankfully, we were starting to see the fruits of his labours. The players he'd found for us, such as Christian Romero, Rodrigo Bentancur and Dejan Kulusevski had helped us finish in the top 4 – and above Arsenal again for the seventh consecutive season - and with the likes of Ivan Perisic, Richarlison, Fraser Forster, Yves Bissouma, Clement Lenglet, Destiny Udogie and Djed Spence coming in, it looked like we had spent big and well yet again as there was sufficient talent to cover all bases as the club embarked on its first Champions League campaign in three seasons. Although the latter signing Conte was keen to stress was a "club signing" in a possible nod to Levy getting involved where he wasn't welcome again.

Once again, we started well. All barring our opening day 4-1 victory over Southampton, we were waiting for the side to click into gear, despite amassing seven wins and one defeat (away to the Scum) we sat third. We also escaped the Champions League group stages with a memorable win at Marseille but every game felt hard going for Spurs. We were all waiting for the team to gel and click and whilst Tottenham podcasts and my friends alike were all saying the same thing, "We're winning while we play bad, that's a mark of a great team" and other such cliches, we were deluding ourselves.

Conte's tactics looked outdated and had taken the shine of the previous season's Golden Boot winner

Heung-Min Son. He looked half the man we knew he could be and while Harry Kane was still doing the business for us, his strike partner looked lost.

Were the players saving themselves for the World Cup in Qatar that was to break up their season? We hoped so but then tragedy struck. Fitness coach, Gian Piero Ventrone, a long-term friend of Conte's, passed away after a short illness. His death was sudden and had a profound effect on the Italian, who also suffered two further bereavements in his life in quick succession, including former Italy teammate Gianluca Vialli. The gaffer was suffering physically too as it was announced that he was having trouble with his gall bladder, resulting in a break from leading the side whilst he flew back to Italy to have it removed. Christian Stellini was installed in his place and he oversaw victories over Manchester City, in which Kane broke Jimmy Greaves's all-time goalscoring record in a 1-0 win, then the first league victory over Chelsea in four years.

But Conte was at breaking point. He rushed himself back and we limped out embarrassingly in the FA Cup in a giant-killing away to Championship side Sheffield United. Fans were in uproar as a side that still sat in 4th place in March was still more boring to watch than arguably, we had been since the George Graham days.

Conte, like Mourinho before him, just didn't fit our ethos and despite Levy's pledge to the fans that he wanted a manager to bring our traditional attacking football back to N17, Conte was yet another big-name appointment, great for club profile, but not for morale inside the club itself. Who can forget his regimental-like pre-season regimes where he had the players running from one side of the pitch to the other until they threw up? Or the 2km run he'd make them all do before a game? I'm surprised that bloke from Full Metal Jacket didn't take over as our fitness coach. We thought it was making the players fitter. What it did was make them more tired for the games coming up. I bet even Dave Mackay would have puked in his training bib.

After the January signing of Pedro Porro from Sporting Lisbon and an awful 4-1 defeat away to Leicester, in which Bentancur did his ACL and was going to be out for the rest of the season, Conte and his side limped on until late March when a 3-3 draw away to Southampton set Conte raging. His press conference, and what he said, was truly explosive.

He questioned the mentality of the club, saying that we are not used to playing for something important or not wanting to play under stress and pressure. He made out, not for the first time, that he was above us. He questioned his chairman, his players, everything. Given half the chance he'd probably have moaned about the quality of food in the canteen given the depth of his tirade. I implore you, if you are brave enough that is, to watch the entire presser on YouTube. We had no idea, due to his contract situation, if he'd be there past the summer. Now we knew that he wouldn't even make it through Spring.

Then came the moment in the Champions League last 16-second leg at home to AC Milan. At a rain-sodden Tottenham Hotspur Stadium, already 1-0 down from the previous leg, Conte substituted defender Davinson Sanchez on, much to the visible annoyance of coach Ryan Mason and Harry Kane, as when Spurs needed a goal in a very winnable game, the Italian was sabotaging his job and throwing the team under the bus in the process by forcing them to stick to his robust, inflexible defensive tactics. The crowd booed loudly and the mood was flat and desperate. We lost, Cristian Romero was sent off and it was a miserable night to be a Spurs fan again.

Conte was given his marching orders the following day after bringing the club into disrepute. The last we saw of him was a photo of him sitting on an Easyjet flight back home. Despite getting us top 4 the previous year, it was good riddance to a man who, despite maybe laying down some home truths, had dismantled any good feeling between him and the club.

Around this time, Fabio Paratici was banned from football globally for 30 months, pending a criminal investigation for financial malpractice. Then Levy employed Stellini as our first team coach and kept all of Conte's staff on the books. That was until a truly humiliating 6-1 defeat at Newcastle, in which we went down 5-0 in 20 minutes and Hugo Lloris didn't come out for the second half, having been subbed after ripping into his teammates at half-time, thus bringing a close to his incredible service to the club.

Stellini and all the staff were roundly dismissed after this and we soldiered on again with Ryan Mason in charge but this time there was to be no Europe qualification. In the final ten games of the season, we fell out of the top 4 and finished 8th, our lowest finish since 2008-09 having conceded 63 goals, the fifth worst in the league. Harry Kane, in his last season as a Spur, grabbed 32 goals but the team was broken and the fans once again were tired of the same shit happening over and over again.

In the final home matches of the season, fans started audibly calling for Levy's head. In the twenty-two years since he and ENIC had taken over, the club had indeed risen higher than they had ever been before in the Premier League years but a catalogue of bad decisions had seen the tide turn well and truly against him.

We had no manager, no director of football, our best player was on his way out of the club and our captain was nowhere to be seen. Let's not forget too that West Ham won their first trophy in 43 years. Under David Moyes. In Europe. The same Europa Conference League we thought we were above the season before this one, just to make things feel worse. And what made things even worse was that for a large chunk of the season, it looked like the Gooners were going to win the league until they bottled a record lead to Man City. Should have written a book about that instead, might have cheered me up a bit...

So there we have it, we've made it you and I, at the other end after getting through the awful times that our beloved club has thrown at us, in one way or another, over the past three decades.

And I didn't use the word "Spursy" once.
Ah...

9

WORST SIGNINGS

Or the worst players and those who were signed at the wrong time...

Let's face it. Every single professional footballer who has ever made it is several thousand times better than your average Joe like me and possibly you. I don't know, I've never seen you do one hundred keepy-uppies or bang one in the top corner from 30 yards, so who am I to judge? Who's anyone? Well, a wise person once said that everybody is a critic and so on that basis, we can all get stuck in on the players who ruined a perfectly good afternoon or evening of football.

When our hard-earned cash goes on travel, tickets, beers and pies and seeing our friends and loved ones, whether it be at the game or down the pub, you don't want some highly paid doofus putting through his own net or pulling an attacker down in the last minute of a game or missing a sitter even your double amputee Grandad could stick in, do you? And that's why football-y inept so 'n' so's like I can holler at someone who is having to perform to a high standard in front of thousands and who is just trying to do his job. Albeit badly.

So that being said, the opinions I am about to share are not those of anyone else but myself and I am not meaning to do down the individual personally. Whether it was injury, confidence issues, being played out of position or being signed by a manager who leaves soon after, there's always good reason why someone doesn't cut it at a club.

Then again, they might just be really crap.

So, in no particular order, here we go. The eleven worst signing and players I've seen stink up our beloved Tottenham...

Paulinho – 2013-2015
Club Appearances: 67
Club Goals: 10

The first player through the door in the summer of 2013, Paulinho's stock was high. Despite having never played in Europe, the Brazil International was a quality box-to-box midfielder, who at a club record fee of £17m looked more than ready to take the Premier League by storm. Pundits and fans were purring over the prospect of seeing him in a midfield three of Moussa Dembele and Sandro and early signs were good, obtaining himself a Man of the Match award on his debut against Crystal Palace. His first goal for the club came in the Europa League but his most memorable contribution was a last-minute backheel winner away to Cardiff that September.

Within months both his and Spurs' form began to tank and by December, manager Andre Villas-Boas was replaced by Tim Sherwood, who preferred to blood youngster Nabil Bentaleb in his place and Paulinho had to make do with bit-part appearances for the rest of the season. Come 2014-15, the Brazilian, who featured in his country's embarrassing 7-1 loss to Germany in that summer's World Cup, never seemed to be in new manager Mauricio Pochettino's plans either and after another lacklustre season, was shipped out the following summer to the Chinese Super League after 30 appearances and 2 goals in all competitions.

I desperately wanted Paulinho to work. A friend at Goal, the football website I worked for at the time, described Paulinho as, "a bit like Jermaine Jenas, only better." Rarely have I ever felt as lied to as I did then. With a dearth of talent and more dependency form-wise, and three managers in two seasons, maybe Paulinho was always doomed to fail. How the heck did he end up having a career at Barcelona, by the way!?

Roberto Soldado – 2013-2015
Club Appearances: 76
Club Goals: 16

Speaking of desperately wanting someone to succeed, Roberto Soldado comes top of that list. With Bale on his way to Madrid, we spent a large chunk of the £85.5m coming in on a Spanish import who promised so much. Breaking our transfer record of £26m, big things were expected. Having scored 24 goals in La Liga the previous season, Soldado excited many and the Spain International began to repay our faith with four goals in his first three games in our colours, even if two of them were penalties.

His link-up play with other attackers was really good too, but after a lean period of games all confidence drained from Roberto and he quickly became a shadow of his former self. On the rare occasion he did score, his celebrations were always more about relief and surprise. He always had the backing of the Spurs fans, even after terrible, game-costing misses, including one against Burnley in the cup that was harder to miss than score.

Like his fellow Magnificent Seven teammates he struggled for form and when Harry Kane began to find more game time and his goals started to flow, Soldado dropped from first choice to third up front, falling behind the enigma that was Emmanuel Adebayor too.

After an unhappy two years in North London, Soldado departed for Villareal and overhit his kicking of a football into his new fans at his unveiling. He also left behind the embarrassing footage of him hitting the post from point-blank range after Ryan Mason's long-range strike against Nottingham Forest to warm our hearts. Sorry, it didn't work out, Roberto.

Gilberto – 2008-2009
Club Appearances: 7
Club Goals: 1

In the war of the North London clubs, both have had Gilbertos on their side. Unsurprisingly, for us, we got the dud.

A £1.9m acquisition from Hertha Berlin, left-back Gilberto holds the distinction of being the first Brazilian to play for our great club. Unfortunately for him, he also turned out to be one of the worst in our history.

The former Brazil International (!) did little to endear himself to supporters when his back pass set up the only goal in our 1-0 defeat to PSV in the UEFA Cup, although he did score his only goal for the club against West Ham a few days later. In truth, he didn't look suited to the Premier League, was prone to lapses in concentration and injury (his debut against PSV came nearly two months after he signed) and Juande Ramos even took him off just 45 minutes into that first appearance, later citing it was because he was still recovering from injury and not because of his error.

By the 2008-09 season, Gilberto only made three appearances for us before having his contract terminated by mutual consent and returning to his native Brazil.

Tanguy Ndombele – 2019-2024
Club Appearances: 91
Club Goals: 10

If I had a pound every time, I heard someone say, "There's a player in Ndombele" I'd be a rich man. The current club record (do you see a trend here?) signing at a costly £55.5m from Lyon was the first big signing following our Champions League final defeat to Liverpool and Spurs fans were jubilant, having seen the Frenchman turn it on in that competition the previous year.

What we got, however, was a homesick player, who had issues with his fitness and who has had six managers in his five years on the books at Tottenham. Ndombele started brightly, scoring on his debut in a 3-1 win over Aston Villa but his time at the club had been marred by ill-discipline off the pitch.

It's a massive shame. We were hoping that Tanguy would plug the hole left by Moussa Dembele and there have been flashes of brilliance in which he's shown us that, with enough application, he could still have a career at the club. It was only under Josè Mourinho that we saw what he was capable of with a delicious lobbed goal over Sheffield Utd being a notable highlight. Yet, with his lack of pressing game highlighted famously by Jamie Carragher at Sky, and so many people having tried to motivate him (that toe-curling scene in All or Nothing when even Daniel Levy gives it a try) it seemed that Ndombele's biggest enemy was himself.

Following a lacklustre game in the FA Cup third round against Morecambe, when he slowly trudged off the pitch and was booed by his fans for not getting a move on, Ndombele hasn't played a competitive game for Spurs since and after seasons out on loan with old club Lyon and Napoli, it seems no one has wanted to take him on either.

Ndombele failed to impress Ange Postacoglou in pre-season before the 2023-24 season and was shipped out again to Galatasaray, where Spurs fans were alarmed by a photo posted on social media of the

Frenchman looking very overweight while playing in Turkey. A sad sight for all of us who had high hopes for the lad.

Ian Walker – 1989-2001
Club Appearances: 313
Club Goals: 0

There's probably a decent amount of you reading this book (I hope) who probably think that I'm being unfair to Ian Walker. For a decade, his floppy haircut and model good looks appeared season upon season at White Hart Lane, spending most of it as club number one after sharing some time between the sticks with cult hero, Erik Thorsevedt. So, why do I classify a man who made over 300 appearances for us and even won a trophy at the club as one of the worst to play for us? Especially given the teams he played in over the years?

Yes, there aren't many individual howlers that spring to mind, at least not for us, but Walker was the embodiment of the mediocrity that had sunk into the club in the 1990s. I can't help but look at him and think of all those awful seasons in which we were almost relegated or finished low enough in the table to not trouble anybody. My overwhelming memory of Walker was of him getting a hand to a shot or header but not doing enough to stop it from going in, then picking himself off the turf and wearing a disgusted look on his face as his hands were placed unhappily on his hips. He wore that expression so often that I'm surprised it didn't become his permanent face.

I didn't rate him. Neither did my friends. After seeing what Espen Baardsen could do, we were convinced he should be the number one, not Walker. That's how bad we were! Yes, he did play in sides where he had to keep the goal behind a defence made up of names who should be on this list too, were it not for more expensive signings. Ramon Vega, John Scales, Paolo Tramezzani, Stuart Nethercott to name but a few but that's no excuse. He didn't keep a clean sheet in the Prem for a year!

Even when he got the chance for England, in one of four of his caps, he cost us the game in a crucial qualifier against Italy, when he let Gianfranco Zola's shot past him at the near post. Why we never looked to upgrade him is a mystery to me. When Neil Sullivan finally did displace Walker, who left for Leicester the following year, the Scotsman was statistically the third-best keeper for shots saved that season. Walker had no way back. Hooray!

Clinton Njie – 2015-2016
Club Appearances: 14
Club Goals: 0

It was a toss-up between Njie and George Kevin Nkoudou as to who I included on this list, both having been signed around the same time. Yet while I remember Nkoudou doing something for us, Njie, well, didn't. Okay, maybe I'm being a bit flippant there. He did set Lamela away for our fourth in a memorable victory over Man City, he was a youngster signed by Mauricio Pochettino for £8.3m from Lyon.

A tricky winger, the future Cameroon International's progress at the club was halted when he suffered an MCL tear early in his career and after that? Well, this was around the time that we were going from strength to strength and in his one season at the club he was restricted to just eight appearances in the league, all coming from the bench.

Within a year he was out on loan to Marseille, who eventually bought him from us at the end of that deal and he built a career back in France, showing that it was probably all a bit too soon for Njie to make the big step up to the Premier League.

He was bloody good on FIFA if you stuck with him though!

Bobby Zamora – 2003-2004
Club Appearances: 18
Club Goals: 1

Lethal during Brighton's rise from the fourth tier to the Championship, Booby Zamora had been trailed for two years by Glenn Hoddle and was seen as one of, if not the best, player outside the Premier League in the country. It looked a steal when Hoddle convinced the young striker to join his new-look front line at Spurs when we stumped up £1.5m for him.

It turned out to be a bad move for Zamora, who despite a goal against future side West Ham to knock them out of the League Cup, failed to make a starting place his own. He looked out of his depth, like this move was too soon in his young career. Yet, his biggest contribution to Spurs wasn't on the pitch.

In January 2004, he was a part of the deal that saw Jermain Defoe join us from the Hammers. It was a move that worked out for both of them as Defoe became a legend for us and Zamora became a favourite at Upton Park and later at QPR.

Vincent Janssen – 2016-2019
Club Appearances: 42
Club Goals: 6

Another example of a player looking red hot and then Tottenham turning them to cold turkey. Janssen, at 22 and having been the Eredivisie top scorer with AZ Alkmaar the previous campaign, looked like just what we needed when Harry Kane was either resting or injured. Pochettino was beaming with joy when we got him, saying that he has all the attributes we needed but, in all fairness, Janssen was never up to the standard required in the Premier League and following the form of Heung-Min Son that season, he barely saw a look in as we finished second in the table.

A season out on loan followed in which he was carted off to Fenerbache and the following season he didn't make an appearance until April due to injury and Poch, seeing the error of his ways, did not even fancy him. A missed chance against West Ham, in our first defeat in the new stadium, and he was gone and is by now just a bad not-so-distant memory for us Spurs fans.

Bongali Khumalo – 2011-2015
Club Appearances: 0
Club Goals: 0

The most pointless signing in the history of the club. In 2011, ENIC signed a partnership with a South African club named SuperSport United and Khumalo was seemingly forced on manager at the time Harry Redknapp, who didn't rate the defender, had him on the bench a couple of times and then loaned him out to Preston.

He never played for us, spent four and a half years on our books and was generally a waste of space. Pointless. Moving on.

Helder Postiga – 2003-2004
Club Appearances: 24
Club Goals: 2

In 2003, with Teddy Sheringham, Les Ferdinand and Steffen Iversen all having left the club, Glenn Hoddle was looking for attackers to play with Robbie Keane and in the Portuguese Postiga, he thought he'd found a gem. A £6.25m signing from Porto, Hoddle purred, "He is a player who will add definite striking quality to our squad and is a young player of proven ability. I'm sure our supporters will enjoy watching him over the coming seasons."

Whatever faith healer, the infamous Eileen Drewery had worked into Hoddle's mind, it was badly misplaced as misfiring Helder only scored one Premier League goal for us before returning to his former club.

His manager Josè Mourinho had been happy to sell Postiga to Spurs, despite admitting he wasn't so sure it was the best move for him and our future manager turned out to be right.

Of course, he had to score the equaliser against England in our quarter-final showdown at Euro 2004, didn't he? And bury a penalty in the shoot-out that helped knock us out...

Grezgorz Rasiak – 2005-2006
Club Appearances: 9
Club Goals: 0

Rasiak was a £3m purchase from Derby County. Having a good scoring record in the second tier, manager Martin Jol wanted Rasiak as a further option behind Robbie Keane, Jermain Defoe and Mido. On his transfer, Jol said that he was, a tall target man, a hard-working, honest player with a good goal-scoring record". It read more like a character evaluation and did little to inspire the White Hart Lane faithful.

On his debut against Liverpool, he had a goal disallowed as Michael Carrick's corner had swung out of play and really, that's the last time he troubled any of our opponent's defences.

Sure there were a lack of chances for game time, and by February Rasiak had returned to the Championship, this time on loan to Southampton, who he later joined permanently and had a successful time on the South Coast.

Despite his lack of game time, Rasiak looked like a fish out of water in our side, who were pushing for a

Champions League place that season. He didn't look strong and lacked any synchronicity with Keane or Defoe. He was like me playing up front. That's not a good thing!

My Worst Tottenham Premier League Eleven:

Ian Walker

Bongali Khumalo Ricardo Rocha Stuart Nethercott

Paulinho

Clinton Njie Tanguy Ndombele (c) Gilberto

Helder Postiga Grezgorz Rasiak Vincent Janssen

10

WORST MATCHES

The heartbreak, the moments that have denied us glory and the ones that opposition fans just love to remind us about. Are we unlucky? Cursed? Sp***y? Let's find out...

Liverpool 2-0 Tottenham - Champions League Final – 2018-19

The ultimate heartbreaker.

The most crushing defeat in my lifetime as a Spurs fan and the one that confirmed to me that dreams don't come true if you support Tottenham. The biggest game in the club's history, perhaps the only time we would fly close to ultimate glory and it was all spoilt after 24 seconds.

Liverpool, who had suffered an embarrassing loss in the final the previous season to a Gareth Bale-inspired Real Madrid, were outright favourites and caught us out immediately when Sadio Mane saw Moussa Sissoko pointing at a teammate and aimed the ball right at the Frenchman's outstretched arm from point blank range. The ball hit his chest then bounced up onto his arm and by the letter of the law, the referee gave a penalty. Mohammad Salah slotted the ball past Hugo Lloris and we never recovered, eventually conceding again to Divok Origi's low shot in the final minutes to condemn us to defeat.

The sense of injustice at that penalty decision was such that FIFA ultimately changed the laws in the weeks after the final, meaning that Spurs had once again been used as guinea pigs for another bullshit rule change. I'm still fuming. I might never get over this game and it's no exaggeration to say that I don't think I felt happy being a Tottenham fan again until around the time Conte joined. It sucked all the joy and life out of me. That day I'd been to a suit fitting for my upcoming wedding so I had a gathering back at my house after but I wasn't much in the way of good company in those 90 minutes and was even worse afterwards. I was inconsolable. I couldn't sleep that night, even after the watching party (including me, my wife-to-be, her Evertonian Father, my Liverpool-supporting best man and my West Ham friend) had left or gone to bed. Even a consolation hug from the victorious best man didn't console me. Liverpool had got their way again. I've never seen the game back, only an image of the Sissoko handball for this book.

The repercussions were soon felt. Why had Pochettino dropped Lucas Moura after his hat-trick in the previous round against Ajax? Why did he go for an unfit Harry Kane, who did not influence the game? Would Lucas have made a difference? If that penalty hadn't been given would we have played better? In the end, it's all ifs and buts and ultimately there's no way we will ever know.

The best of frenemies – Kamruz and I just before the Champions League final, 2019

Tottenham 3-4 Manchester City – FA Cup Fourth Round – 2003-04

As a fourteen-year-old, Tottenham were my biggest obsession. I had well over 40 (yes, I counted them) posters all over my wall, ripped out of issues of Spurs Monthly and Match, plus a solitary Holly Valance pin-up to make it look like I wasn't totally in love with all the men on my wall. But after this defeat, the tide started to turn somewhat. My experience as a fan had heralded nothing but disappointment and this result took the biscuit.

It looked promising at the start, though. My Dad picked me up from my school friend's house (he was an Ipswich Town fan, so sympathised with my pain constantly) and as we were making the drive back home we heard alerts on Five Live for Ledley King's opener, Robbie Keane's doubler and just as I raced upstairs to turn my radio on, Christian Ziege's free-kick that put us three goals up.

You know the rest, and I wrote about the devastating second half elsewhere in the book (see Worst Seasons – 2003-04) but it's fair to say that I wasn't happy and that alarm radio clock sadly didn't see it through the night.

Tottenham 3-5 Manchester United – Premier League – 2001-02

The original capitulation and humiliation. In September 2001, both clubs had started auspiciously, with us settling into life with a new 3-5-2 attacking system under Glenn Hoddle and champions Manchester United trying to find the form that had seen them romp to yet another League title the previous season and still reeling from the departure of Jaap Stam. Despite that, they still had heavy hitters in the side with Rudd Van Nistelrooy and Juan Sebastian Veron adding to a side that was already dripping with talent. And so, as I settled down to watch Final Score at my Nan and Grandad's bungalow in Holland-on-Sea, Essex, I darted around the place when debutant and £8m signing Dean Richards headed us into an early lead. I nearly blew the roof off when Les Ferdinand doubled our advantage. I had to be restrained from taking all my clothes off and running into the garden naked with joy when Christian Ziege made sure that we went in at the break THREE goals up!

Then, it was home time. My sisters were much younger than me (I was 12, they were 9 and 2) and so we had to be getting back home. As we feverishly tuned into Five Live for the hour-long journey home my world fell apart just as quickly as Tottenham's defence that day. Andy Cole got one back almost immediately after the break. Then new signing Laurent Blanc got United's second. My Dad was still feeling positive but I was getting that queasy feeling...and it wasn't car sickness bringing it on.

By the time we were back home, Van Nistelrooy and Veron had both scored to completely turn around the tie. My Dad was furious and forbade me from switching the TV or the radio on to avoid hearing any football coverage for the rest of the day. He didn't even buy any Sunday papers. It wasn't until I went to school and was roundly laughed at by everybody when I discovered that David Beckham had rubbed salt into the wounds and made it 3-5.

Glenn Hoddle blamed the timing of our third goal for the result. I blamed Glenn Hoddle.

Tottenham 0-2 Portsmouth – FA Cup Semi-final – 2009-10

At the time of writing, we have a terrible record of reaching FA Cup semi's then getting no further. For our previous EIGHT semi-finals, we have lost all of them, stretching back to 1993 when Tony Adams put the Scum through at our expense, then 1995, when we were shocked by an Everton side who went on to lift the trophy. The first one I can remember vividly was losing 2-0 to Newcastle when we should have been awarded a penalty for a blatant handball by Nikos Dabizas, then there was the terrible 2-1 defeat to the Gooners again in 2001.

Fast forward eight years and we were an absolute shoo-in for a place in the final. Our opponents were already relegated and points deducted from Portsmouth who were surely no match for our top 4 chasers.

Watching at home, I couldn't believe my eyes as we somehow failed to score in 90 minutes, despite beingby far the better side. Then lo and behold, what happens? Michael Dawson slipped in the penalty box as he went to clear the ball and Frédéric Piquionne was left with an easy finish as we fell behind to bad luck. Then Peter Crouch had a goal wrongly ruled out for offside before former Spur Kevin-Prince Boateng smashed a penalty in to seal the team in administration into the final at our expense.

My mood wasn't picked up by my then-girlfriend's Dad taunting me down the phone about how many shots we'd had compared to Pompey. I knew he never liked me.

Bayern Munich 1-1 Chelsea – Champions League Final – 2011-12

We all know what happened here and it was a total injustice. Seven years previously Liverpool staged the mother of all comebacks against AC Milan to win their fifth Champions League but they had finished outside the automatic qualification places in the Premier League, pipped to fourth by their bitter rivals Everton. UEFA, reluctant to allow five teams from the same country into their best competition, allowed Liverpool in as holders but they had to start in the first round qualifying campaign in July. After that, it was written into the laws that only four teams should be allowed to compete, at the expense of the fourth-placed side if a team finished outside that but won the competition again.

For most of the season we had looked odds on for the top three but come late winter Harry Redknapp's court case came along and went and just as he was judged not guilty, Fabio Capello resigned from the England job and 'Arry was odds on to take it. Queue a huge media campaign to get him in the hot seat and naturally our season derailed as a consequence. By the time Roy Hodgson was appointed instead, we were out of the FA Cup (see the later entry in this chapter) and needed to win on the final day at home to Fulham and hope Arsenal didn't beat West Brom. There would be no danger of losing CL football in the case that

Chelsea beat Bayern, on their home turf, in the upcoming final.

Chelski has defied the odds, knocking out Barcelona at the Nou Camp in the semis but they had flattered to deceive in the league and under caretaker Roberto Di Matteo they had also qualified for the FA Cup final at our expense but finished tenth in the league.

We won, but so did the Scum, thanks to ex-Spur Marton Fulop throwing two goals in his own net for them. Now it was squeaky bum time for us and we were all praying that Bayern would beat our other fierce London rivals and our 4th place will see us back at Europe's top table next season.

You know what happened next. They beat the Germans on penalties, whilst Harry Redknapp was in the ground watching Spurs being relegated down to the Europa League and knowing that the sack was probably coming his way.

It was. In the next couple of months, Redknapp was gone, Modrić was sold, Ledley retired and we had to rebuild yet again all the while I was cursing the football gods and yelling to the skies that it just wasn't fair.

UEFA agreed and, lo and behold, they scrapped the four teams from one country rule and now we've got a Champions League coming up next season where SIX could represent! Just our luck...

Blackburn Rovers 2-1 Tottenham – Worthington Cup Final – 2001-02

Well, this was all kinds of traumatising as a kid. After our 5-1 tonking of Chelsea in the second leg of the semi-finals our confidence was sky high. Hoddle's new brand of attacking football and a squad with a blend of youth and experience looked like it might see us to instant success but it wasn't to be again. Blackburn took the lead through Matt Jansen after a lucky deflection off Ben Thatcher. We missed chance after chance with Les Ferdinand being guilty of fluffing his lines in front of an in-form Brad Friedel.

We kept plugging away, eventually equalising through Christian Ziege but a Ledley King mistake late on allowed Andy Cole to put us behind again. Gus Poyet then hit the angle of the post and bar when it looked easier to score. Friedel kept us at bay for the rest of the game and was later awarded Man of the Match for his performance but then came a real bone of contention when Teddy Sheringham was tripped in the box.

I was begging, imploring the referee to blow his whistle and give the penalty. A very late equaliser would see us go into extra time and surely pick up another but it wasn't to be. We lost, I bawled my eyes out and my lucky Dad was working a weekend shift and missed the whole bloody thing!

Tottenham 1-2 Manchester United – FA Cup Semi-final – 2017-18

Our second failure at this stage in two seasons, Dele Alli, whose opener briefly put us in the lead, summed it up at the end. "We can't keep doing this," as he despondently shook his head in front of TV cameras.

By full-time, having been well and truly Mourinho'd by the Red Devils, I was having serious deja vu to the previous year when I was eagerly climbing the escalators at Wembley, checking out the team news and sighing as I realised that Pochettino had decided that an FA Cup semi-final was the right time to experiment with his side. But like a teenager who does shrooms before an A-level exam, the FA Cup semi-finals are the wrong time to do it.

"We've got no left back," I said aghast to my friend Nick. The whispers went around the place. "Are we playing three at the back?" "Hazard isn't playing, we don't need a full-back!" said one over-optimistic person. In the end, as the game started we realised, horror of horrors, that Sonny was playing wing-back, gave away a penalty and we lost 4-2.

As I walked into my garden and started aggressively pulling the weeds out of my flower bed, I thought back to that day a year earlier and the quotes I'd seen Poch give in the media. He called the cup competitions, "a distraction" and that winning trophies "only builds egos." Y'know what it also does, Poch? Gives your fans something to cheer about and shuts the rivals and media up about how s****y we are!

So when I saw the team sheet for this I was braced for the worst. Is Harry Kane in goal? Harry Winks up front with Lloris? What crazy arse experimentation was he going to spring on us this time? In the end, it was Michel Vorm who was preferred to our club captain Hugo between the sticks, having been the keeper for the cup run up to this point and Toby Aldewiereld, who had been out for three months earlier in the season, was on the bench and Davinson Sanchez, having had a decent debut season, filled in for him. Victor Wanyama also had to make do with a place on the bench as our side didn't do too badly initially as Dele flossed in front of the Wembley crowd after putting us ahead. But then horror of horrors saw Mousa Dembele hastled off the ball, a sign that his midfield powers were starting to wane, in the build-up to United's leveller. Then Ander Hererra's shot from range went through Vorm's diving hand and we were out again. Josè, who took cups very seriously, beat us and while Spurs fans despaired, Poch was probably slightly relieved that his players' heads were not going to get any bigger.

West Ham 2-1 Tottenham – Premier League – 2005-06

We all know about conspiracy theories but this one, in the pre-social media age, was insane. It was so big a name was given to the pain that we felt that day and that name was Lasagnegate.

It was the biggest day in the club's recent history. On the final day of the season, we faced West Ham, needing to match the Gooner's result in their final game at Highbury against Wigan, to finish in the top 4 and qualify for the Champions League for the very first time. Not since 1962 when it was the European Cup had we dined at the top table of football and we now had the best chance to do so.

The night before the game, the players and staff stayed at the Marriott Hotel, where lasagne was on the menu. That night, several first-team players went down with sickness and diarrhoea. Requests from the Spurs board to reschedule the game fell on deaf ears at the Premier League, whose big wigs were at Highbury that afternoon. Daniel Levy even pushed for a later kick-off time but both the Prem and the Metropolitan Police said no dice.

The first I heard of it was when I checked Ceefax and read that we were trying to get the game cancelled. I read, however, that West Ham were also reluctant to do this as the following weekend they had an FA Cup final to prepare for. Spurs had no friends in high places as the Chief of the Premier League, Richard Scudamore, helping himself to the horderves in the Scum chairman David Dein's director's box, ordered the match to go ahead.

With a team puking and pooing like there was no tomorrow, our brave players went out to face the onslaught of an unsympathetic Upton Park crowd and we fell behind early on, with the likes of Michael Carrick, Edgar Davids, Robbie Keane and Michael Dawson visibly being unwell on the side of the pitch. Jermain Defoe did equalise and as Wigan were beating the Goons, it did momentarily look like we were going to defy the odds but our players were running out of strength. Sadly, the inevitable happened and in the final ten minutes Yossi Benayoun turned in the box and smashed the ball past Paul Robinson and our European dream was over as the Scum were now 4-2 up. Their champagne corks were popping as they were about to have a party over at their gaff, whilst the only thing our boys were going to be cracking out was imodium.

Levy tried to get the game replayed and even asked the police to investigate the Marriott Hotel. Players such as Defoe still swear to this day that someone did something dodgy to their food that night. Match of the Day thought they would be hilarious by putting a photo up of Arsène Wenger in a Chef's outfit, proving that Spurs were trolled en masse long before social media was even a thing. In the end, though, it was a norovirus that had ravaged our squad that day and guess what? The Premier League will allow a game to be rescheduled now if players are poorly. Just ask the Scum themselves...

Looking back now it doesn't feel as heartbreaking as it did then. We've been in the Champions League several times since that horrible day in May 2006 and for the first time since the 1980s, we had qualified for European football through the league. The future still looked bright, even if our changing room that day must have looked like a hideous Jackson Pollock.

I hope an Arsenal fan was hired to clear up the mess...

Tottenham 1-5 Chelsea – FA Cup Semi-final – 2011-12

**** me. Here we go again with another FA Cup semi-final disappointment. This one wasn't so much down to bad luck as much as it felt so bloody unfair. Yes, we were roundly thumped 5-1 but three of them were wonder goals and one never even crossed the line!

Firstly, Harry Redknapp played former blue Carlo Cudicini in goal instead of in-form number one Brad Friedel. Secondly, we played okay in the first half, despite Didier Drogba sending a thumping long-range shot past Cudicini but Juan Mata's "second", which was stopped by Benoit Assou-Ekotto on the line was then given by referee Martin Atkinson in a bizarre moment of controversy. Although we got one back almost instantly through Gareth Bale, the sense of injustice rocked us and Chelski ended up grinding us into the dirt with further goals from Ramires, Frank Lampard and Florent Malouda.

After the match, Harry Redknapp revealed, "I spoke to [the referee] and he said he feels worse than I do about it - I said 'I don't think so.'"

With the ghost goal coming two years after England had been robbed of an equaliser against Germany at the World Cup, the game proved further vindication that goal-line technology was needed in the modern game. Not long after, we got it, but it was too late to help us on that fateful Wembley day.

Dinamo Zagreb 3-0 Tottenham (3-2 agg) – Europa League round of 16 –2020-21

Talk about a game leaving us in turmoil. If one result tells you that the squad had enough of Josè Mourinho, this was it. Having led 2-0 from the first leg and even seen Zagreb manager Zoran Mamic sent to prison for fraud, you'd be forgiven for thinking this was a formality.

How wrong we were. Spurs toiled in both boxes and unravelled spectacularly, being taken to extra time in a game they should have sewn up, not just in the first leg but in normal time. By the time the final whistle was blown, we just knew that the memes, the s****y tag and "Bottlenham Lolspur" were coming our way again and I couldn't feel anything but the sheer familiar feeling of utter disappointment.

"If I forget the last minutes of extra time, where we did something to get a different result and go through, in the 90 minutes and first half of extra time, there was one team that decided to leave everything on the pitch," Mourinho told BT Sport.

"They left sweat, energy, blood. In the end, they left even tears of happiness. Very humble and committed. I have to praise them.

"On the other side, my team. They didn't look like they were playing an important match. If for any one of them, it is not important, for me it is."

He wasn't wrong. The trouble was that Josè had pushed them under the bus so often that by now, they looked like they'd rather humiliate themselves than keep him in a job. They didn't have to wait long for him to be given marching orders by Daniel Levy.

Arsenal 5-2 Tottenham – Premier League – 2011-12

This one stung big time. With ten games to go, victory over a Gooners side who were ten points behind us before kick-off would surely see us finish not only above them but in the Champions League places and replace our bitter rivals in qualification for the competition.

And it started so well, with Louis Saha and an Emmanuel Adebayor penalty putting us a rather undeserved two goals to the good but it didn't take long for us to crumble as goals from Bacary Sagna and Robin Van Persie, who was the only really good player in that Scum side, saw us squander our advantage and go in level at the break.

We looked stunned and at a resurgent Emirates it was the Gooners who came out swinging after the break with the hateful Theo Walcott helping himself to two goals after Tomas Rosicky for his customary goal against us.

The result turned our seasons on their axis. The Gooners went from strength to strength, ultimately pipping us to third on the final day of the season and we looked patchy as rumours about Harry Redknapp's future and uninspiring deadline-day signings like Ryan Nelson and Louis Saha left us weak in the run-in of a season in which we looked like challengers for quite some time.

I sat shell-shocked watching the game at a Spurs mate's house. We both received the same text from the same Gooner friend at the same time. It simply read, "I love football."

I wished that I bloody didn't!

And as a bonus – Chelsea 2-2 Tottenham – Premier League – 2015-16

Okay, I've included this because, well, I can't leave it out really can I? I'll be honest with you though, I wasn't disappointed at the time. I'm not now either, although every time that flipping Eden Hazard equaliser gets shown, I wince like it's a bad memory because in one way it was. It's May 2016 and we are the closest team challenging the anomaly that is Leicester City while all the other big names, many of them in the process of rebuilds, rolled over and had their tummies tickled by the Foxes. But Claudio Ranieri's men hadn't had it all their way.

Lest we forget that the Gooners had been top at Christmas and had even beaten the loathsome Jamie Vardy and his team at the Emirates but by now had slipped to allow us a chance to catch the Foxes. And catch them we nearly did. In fact, by the time Harry Kane and Heung-Min Son had put us two nil up at the break, at a ground that is our infamous bogey stadium, we still needed Leicester to drop points in their remaining two games to realistically win the title.

Sadly, however, Chelsea, who were languishing in mid-table during an off-season, remembered how much they loathed us and conspired to play out of their skins and ended up celebrating the equaliser like they had just won the league themselves!

In the end, a point was enough to see us qualify for the Champions League next season. It was a massive feat for Mauricio Pochettino in just his second season and for such a young, talented side. I was proud of them. While I don't condone violence, I bloody loved how we started treating the Stamford Bridge pitch like it was our prison playground.

With a flurry of dirty tackles, fights erupting on and off the pitch and gouging and studs up in the air, it was all very un-Spurs. This team showed the fight that they had in their veins. Referee Mark Clattenburg seemingly didn't have a handle on the game, despite showing yellow card after yellow card to both sets of players.

"It was theatre," Clattenburg later recalled. "I went in with a gameplan: that I didn't want Tottenham Hotspur blaming Mark Clattenburg that they were losing the title. There should have been three red cards to Tottenham. I allowed them to self-destruct so all the media, all the people in the world went, 'Tottenham lost the title'.

"If I sent three players off from Tottenham, what are the headlines?, 'Clattenburg cost Tottenham the title'. It was pure theatre that Tottenham self-destructed against Chelsea and Leicester won the title."

We ended up being fined £275,000 with Moussa Dembele receiving a six-game ban for appearing to gouge at Diego Costa's face (something Fernando Torres did to Jan Vertonghen two seasons earlier and escaped punishment) whilst our rival's £375,000 fine showed just how much they were sticking it to us too.

In the end, Spurs lost, football won and got its fairytale and we ended up third but let's not forget who the real bottlers were that season...I'm looking at you, Gooners!

11

WORST KITS

As with our best kits, with which I have happy memories and positive thoughts about how they look and feel, these eleven strips are connected to bad memories, negative thoughts and highly opinionated feelings about how they look. Step inside the wardrobe that time wished it had forgotten.

WARNING – Contains a lot of purple.

2021-22 – Nike third kit

I feel a tiny bit cruel including this one.

Why? It was designed in collaboration with eight local youngsters who attended Tottex, a textiles studio in Seven Sisters Road, and were asked by the Nike Design team to sum up what Tottenham means to them.

The club's press release stated that:

"The group's creative vision has now been brought to life with the Third Kit design encompassing bold prints and patterns inspired by the streets of Tottenham. The striking purple design celebrates the vibrancy of the Club's N17 neighbourhood, with an N17 logo on the inside collar."

Sadly, it looked as though Nike had chosen a team of kids who supported the wrong side in North London as the horrific mixture of purple and green looked like the sort of bad acid flashback a hippie from the 60s would have.

Sure, we had a few notable games in it, an emphatic 4-0 demolition of Leeds on the road and a late 1-0 win over Watford and, well, that's pretty much it.

There's just too much going on to make it look credible. Less is more, that's what I say.

1995-96 – Pony away kit

Again, you'd be forgiven for thinking that I have something against purple kits, and in a way, you'd be right. Following on from the previous season's iconic Holsten away strip (think Klinsmann's dive at Hillsborough) our new kit manufacturer, Pony, wanted to emulate a similarly iconic design and got it wrong.

A strange two-tone of purple and navy shades, encompassed by the huge badge and cockerel that our shirts had at this point and it looked like we had ten outfield players who were all having a kickabout after riding in the 1.10 at Ascot.

Still, at least we didn't clash with our opponents, who were probably all too busy laughing at us to turn up and beat us. Maybe that's why we almost qualified for Europe this season. Maybe that's the secret to success. Crap kits!! Hell, if we'd worn this for our home strip maybe we'd have won the league?!

Okay, I'll calm down now.

I know Pony were our manufacturers but did they really have to make our players look like jockeys? In an era where there were so many memorable strips in football, ours seemed to start to look like people were just trying to make us look silly. Indeed, it's a joke among fans of a certain vintage that the kit manufacturers at this time summed up our football too. Let's not get started on the following season's custard cream kit...

1999-00 Adidas away kit

I probably shouldn't admit this but when Adidas took over from Pony at the end of the millennium, I thought our new shirts for the 1999-00 season were a massive step up in quality. Sure, I associate the strips with boring football and the final days of Ginola and NAME REDACTED, but as time has worn on, my love has slipped somewhat for one kit in particular and I'm afraid it's this one.

We've had blue and yellow away kits in the past and Adidas thought it would be a good idea to combine them both in a not-so-subtle way. The navy blue with the yellow chest and back and the three-lined Adidas trademark complete with white collar and white shorts again looked like it belonged in another sport.

The kit was given an update in 2001-02 when it was worn for our League Cup final defeat at the hands of Blackburn Rovers, since both our home kit and our sky-blue away kit that season clashed with the white and blue strip of our opponents (though there had been no such problem in our early season encounter at Ewood Park.)

It's not as abhorrent or offensive to the eye as some of the other kits on this list, nor do I compare it to traumatic defeats or moments in my life as a Spurs fan (barring that final, but that was just a retread) but it's too busy, too vulgar and a reminder that not all 90s kits are that loveable and iconic.

2013-14 Under Armour home kit

I've always thought that you can't go too wrong with a home kit. No matter how many times they try to jazz it up with a go-faster stripe or stinky yellow stains under the armpits (too many good memories associated with that kit, so no way that's going on this list) but some can end up having a negative feeling attached to them for several reasons. Poor results, certain players wearing it, a bad time in the club's - or indeed your own personal – history and all of a sudden, a kit can seem a bit whiffy.

The open collar skin-tight Under Armour effort for the 2013-14 season, is such a kit. It epitomises that nomadic era between our highs of the Redknapp days and what was to come under Pochettino and whether the boys were lining up in the HP or AIA sponsor (the latter was for cup ties) it's blank, almost retro design sums up a brief period in which we felt like nomads again.

This is the kit that Gareth Bale was photoshopped into wearing that was plastered above Times Square. Yet, aside from one pre-season friendly, he never appeared in a competitive game in it. It was also the kit which saw our magnificent seven largely put in very mediocre performances.

The team itself, led by Andre Villas-Boas then Tim Sherwood, were thrashed thoroughly by all our big rivals that season and so memories are far from fond with this one.

Next!

2005-06 Kappa away kit

In a precursor to our 2009/10 season home kit, Kappa were the first kit manufacturer to introduce yellow armpit stains to N17. Why they thought it would be a good idea, I don't know, especially as they ditched our traditional navy blue colours for a more royal blue shade that resembled the seats at White Hart Lane at the time.

My overriding memory of us in this one was the embarrassing 1-0 away defeat to Grimsby in the League Cup second round, a 2-0 away defeat to Bolton and, in a rare win in this kit, a 2-1 win at Wigan, where Edgar Davids scored his only goal in this appalling strip.

When my father changed jobs his work colleagues decided to gift him this kit in an XL, which always left me wondering whether the company he was working for either didn't know him well or possibly didn't like them.

He never wore it but I did and despite me being a large size at the worst, it still clung to me like that alien symbiote in Venom. It was suffocating, like cling film over my mouth and it reeked of failure. I hated it. Thankfully we didn't wear it much.

Still got it though, for my sins.

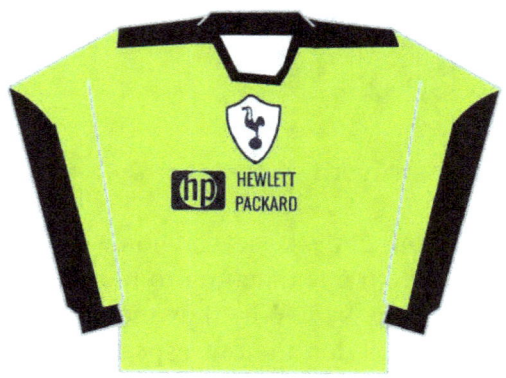

1995-96 Pony goalkeeper kit

I felt so tempted to put all our kits in from this season, Pony's first in charge as our kit manufacturers, but the home kit misses out just on the basis that it's more boring than offensive to my eyes. This kit is definitely the latter.

It was bought for me by a Chelsea-supporting friend when I was 12. He saw it on a market stall and initially I was thrilled...until I saw it. Once seen it definitely cannot be seen, that's for sure.

It was a bright, dayglow, luminous green.

Looking back, it felt cruel to put Ian Walker in this kit. How could the opposition miss? If the stadium lights failed at White Hart Lane, he'd still be seen. From space. It could power the National Grid! It looked nuclear! It's my least favourite shirt of all time, worn by my least favourite keeper of all time.

Yet did that stop me from wearing it? Nope. It was quilted so kept me warm when throwing myself between the sticks onto the frozen muddy ground at school and down the park.

Still, it's an abomination and more of a stain on our name than that time we tried to move to Stratford.

The yellow alternative wasn't much better!

1997-99 Pony goalkeeper kit

A slight improvement on its predecessor, but still terrible. Seemingly inspired by David Seaman's crazy

England Euro 96 kits, this orange, yellow, dark and bright blue effort was...well...crap.

Okay, it is the strip that Walker wore when we won the Worthington Cup but it's also stained with the threat of relegation in 1998 and my memory of Walker, Espen Baardsen, Frode Grodas and Han Segers and the shambles that we were defensively back then.

Far inferior to the more subtle green alternative kit, it hurt my eyes having to look at it. It is the embodiment of garish, gaudy 90s designs that I know some people love now but not me.

It makes me want to be colour-blind.

2022-23 Nike away kit

Bloody hell.

Again, tied to a season of unbridled disappointment, the camp scuba diving look might look fine on the catwalk or in some night clubs but in the early 2020s, not so much on the football field.

When it came out, it became instantly meme-able, by both self-defacing Spurs fans and rivals. In an era where hits now cost over £100, what did Nike think they were playing at? Purple (again!), black sleeves with luminous polo neck collar and trim, it sucked big time, said nothing about our club or our traditions and looked like someone at Nike was having a laugh. I mean, people get paid good money to come up with this shit!

To quote The Simpsons "I really hope that someone got fired for this blunder." As it's the last kit Harry Kane wore in the Premier League in our 4-1 away win at Elland Road, it spoilt the last competitive game of arguably our greatest-ever player and that simply isn't on.

We also wore it when Sheffield United dumped us out of the FA Cup.

Truly awful.

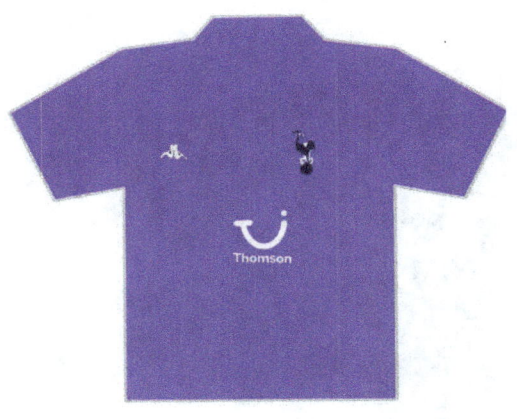

2003-04 Kappa purple kit

Some things in life are just inevitable. Death, taxes and awful Kappa kits at Tottenham. With 2003-04 having nothing but negative connotations for me, both the bale blue and all purple away kits were as atrocious as our football that season.

Whilst the blue kit looked like the player's pyjamas or long johns, the purple was just...weird. Sure, earlier on I said that less is more and so just a plain colour across the shirts, shorts and sleeves would suffice but the bright shade of purple just looked like someone had stained our home kit with Ribena.

Add to that the skin-tight nature of our shirts at the time. Any flabby bits on anyone wearing them, which you can get away with in a darker colour (I know I did with the following season's calmer navy kit), but not in something so bright, were on display for all to see. Flattery for the fans was in short supply, on and off the field.

2012-13 Under Armour third kit

I know times were a bit depressing after Chelsea won the Champions League and relegated us to the Europa League, and when Luka Modrić left us, but to dress our players up in a black and grey kit felt like they were in mourning.

We all were after our second consecutive 5-2 mauling away to the Scum and we were wearing this kit. Under Armour's designs were a little bland to say the least, (although the navy-blue away strip for this season was rather lovely), and uninspiring compared to the Puma strips we'd had from 2006-2012 but maybe they were overreaching with this one.

Apart from a 1-0 win over West Brom at the Hawthorns, I can't remember us winning much when we wore it and thankfully we didn't wear it alot but it does hold a slightly special place for some people as it coincided with Bale's explosive form taking off.

To me it was dreary and lacking any colour whatsoever, something you would never accuse our Welsh wizard of being and I hated looking at it every time we wore it.

I mean, who wears an away kit for the North London derby anyway?

2023-24 Nike third kit

A late admission in this list but a worthy one at that considering, at the time of writing, there are some sectors of Spurs' social media blaming this taupe design for being instrumental in our surprising 4-0 drubbing at Newcastle.

Evoking memories of the grey Manchester United kit that Alex Ferguson infamously made them change at half-time back in the 90s, they might have a point. This taupe number was worn in our early season elimination from the Carabao Cup, our 1-0 win at Luton, a 4-2 humbling at Brighton and our entertaining 3-3 draw up at the Etihad against Man City and every time, it looked like our boys were streaking on the pitch!

Whether or not the colour of the kit contributed to two heavy defeats in games we were favoured to win, we just don't know, but same as the previous entry, the colour isn't standard Tottenham, it's boring to look at and has negative connections to embarrassing results.

12

VILLAINS

Those that we love to hate. The people and things that have given me the right hump over the Premier League years. Irredeemable, unloved, hateful and guaranteed to bring a bit of bile bubbling up your throat when you think of them.

Judas Iscariot

Whatever has been said in the past about this man doesn't need saying again, to be honest. With the poor taste terrace songs, the social media hate, and the abuse he still receives from Spurs fans over two decades after he made his decision to cross the great divide, rival fans must be asking why we can't just let it go.

Well, several reasons. Firstly, he was our club captain. Secondly, he deliberately ran his contract down and kept his true plans secret, depriving the club of a signing fee which would have seen us able to spend more money on shoring up a defence that back then was as rusty as a spitfire left in a field for eighty years.

Also, for years he was remorseless. Didn't he realise how many young children looked up to him? Also, he was our best player. He made their side better. He won things we were dreaming of winning, with them!

I don't condone the songs nor do I sing them but do I forgive? Not at all. Do I forget? Never.

VAR

You know the moments when something has happened off the ball or the final cross into the box finds a player who looked onside but the ref or linesman didn't see it? That's why Video Assistant Referees were introduced at the end of the 2010s so that "clear and obvious" errors could be looked at again on a screen on the side of the pitch with a referee in a booth somewhere telling the match official what to look for. What was voted for unanimously by the Premier League, however, has ended up causing more debate and more acrimony for every single side.

Although it has given us some very sweet moments and helped us to victory on occasion (Llorente's goal and Eriksen's suicidal back pass in the Champions League) it's also deprived us on more than one occasion and arguably ended up costing us more points than we'd have won if the referees didn't have it.

Anyone who listened to the audio of the hilariously wrong Luis Diaz incident at our place in 2023-24 would come to the same conclusion. Too many cooks. If I had that many voices in my head, I'd be in psychiatric care so I really don't know how the referees cope.

I don't know any fan who likes it and it dominates football now in a negative way, leading me nicely on to my next choice.

PGMOL

Remember that little child who used to be picked last when you'd play football in the playground? The utterly hopeless who and you put in goal, only for the bigger kids to smash the ball at them until they cried? Well, that little boy or girl went on to be a referee, who delighted in ruining everyone's weekend and when they retire, they end up working for the PGMOL.

The Professional Game Match Officials Limited has always been there in the background in one form or another like some kind of loathsome illuminate and since the introduction of VAR, it has been forced to make dozens of public apologies for mistakes made in big games. However, although some high-profile controversies have come out in favour of mistakes made against Spurs, none so far have come out to explain why some decisions were made and some not. It's almost as though the managers who kick and scream about it most (Klopp, Arteta etc) can manipulate it to their desire and lo and behold they get some decisions going their way and why? Because the PGMOL is a smug, biased, shallow and allegedly corrupt governing body. Just ask Mark Halsey...

Plus, Howard Webb is in charge of it. No wonder Manchester United get so many penalties.

Sky Sports

It's the beast that creates a monster. For all the good Sky has done for English football it's also at the root of all that's gone wrong with it. The money, the sanitised game, the ridiculous subscription fees. Most fans around the country think that Sky Sports have an agenda against them and it's almost 100% true that there isn't one but in the social media age, Britain's Premier football provider has started chasing clicks and memes online more than actually giving insightful analysis. Plus, their pundits are biased.

Before you say they are not, why do they have Gary Neville and Jamie Carragher sitting beside each other for Man Utd and Liverpool games, then post clips of their reactions to the match action afterwards? Also, the selection of pundits that they choose from is too top-heavy with clubs that were successful twenty years or so ago. I hate it when they desperately try to sandwich Jamie Redknapp or the now departed Graeme Souness as Spurs players to balance out Carragher and presenter Kelly Cates every time there is a Liverpool-Tottenham game. And Alan Smith, former Arsenal striker, co-commentates on nearly every one of our games! I know TNT Sports has Hoddle, Crouch and Jenas but is there nobody who will stick up for us? I mean they have Michael Dawson, Tim Sherwood and Spurs fan Clinton Morrison in the Soccer Saturday studio. I'd rather see them do more.

Also, Sky Sports have taken the "Spursy" tag and run with it. In 2017, Rachel Riley of Countdown fame was forced to step down when she labelled us "bottle jobs" after our 1-0 defeat to West Ham after an outcry.

Then there's Roy Keane, who is like a rabid dog. You throw him an injured rabbit and he'll rip it to shreds and again, despite being a "Spurs fan", he can be more devastating in his views about us than even the most avid Gooner when we play badly!

The way that Gary Neville sniggered when he talked about us joining the European Super League (a proposal that Sky was livid with so stoked the fire with regards to the outcry as it wouldn't have been the broadcaster of choice) and continues to do us down (calling Ange Postecoglou naive even when we had trounced Neville's darling United 2-0), I swear they don't believe most of the crap they say but as it's good "copy" they are encouraged to ramp it up. Don't get me started on Micah Richards. He was like a loveable enthusiastic puppy when he started but puppies grow up, so when's he going to?

It's always been a bit shit, even in the days of misogynists Richard Keys and Andy Gray. At least they've replaced Martin Tyler, who sounded so unenthused in his job that you'd think they were keeping him animated off a dying car battery with Peter Drury, the poet of the commentating world. Oh no, they've made him hateful now too.

Stay well clear and don't subscribe.

Arsène Wenger

Is it the fact that his appointment not only revolutionised our fiercest rivals but the Premier League also with his fitness and diet methods? Yes. Is it also the fact that the success he had with them happened to coincide with arguably our worst period in the club's recent history? Yes.

Could it just be that I loathe Arsène Wenger because he pinched our club captain and best player from right under our noses? Of course. And that he brought his mob to our gaff to win the Premier League? Of course. That his club's cosiness with the Premier League meant we played the most important game in our history with the shits and lost? Yup.

Might I just possibly hate Arsène Wenger because he managed the Goons for over twenty years and yet despite a nine-year trophy drought managed to end it, two years running, in games against lowly teams like Hull and Aston Villa, while we end up losing our finals to the likes of Man City and United, Chelsea and Liverpool? Most definitely.

It wasn't until near the end of his reign, when he stuck around too long and the Gooners started falling down the league, that I finally began to find him amusing, mainly when remonstrating with a match official or a rival manager.

God, I wish Martin Jol had lumped him.

Theo Walcott and Jack Wilshire

Speaking of annoying tits, nothing winds you up more than members of your rivals' team rubbing it in when your crap. During the 2013-14 season, when we were having our most disappointing campaign in recent times, these two sods wound me up with their lack of decorum and professionalism. Firstly, Theo Walcott, who despite having never played a single minute in the Premier League, somehow dislodged our own Jermain Defoe from England's World Cup squad, decided to wind up our crowd on national television once.

Having been injured in our 2-0 defeat at the Emirates, and carried past the away supporters on the stretcher, Walcott was going to get grief and then decided to mimic the scoreline with his fingers and a sarcastic smug grin all over his face. After that, I hoped it wouldn't be long until someone photoshopped it to reflect back at him the next time we beat the scum. I didn't have to wait too long on that one, thank god.

And as for Wilshire, you've just won your first piece of silverware in nearly a decade, in a match in which you went 2-0 down to Hull City. Indeed, it only took an extra-time winner for you to scrape over the finish line. How do you celebrate at the open-top bus parade? By singing obscene songs about the Spurs into the microphone and getting the fans to sing them back to him. Classy, Jack. I cheered loudly every time he picked up his inevitable injuries in future games against us and the fans didn't forget either.

Having said that, when we win our next trophy, I hope we do nothing but sing songs about that lot down the road. Eye-for-an-eye, and all that.

Jimmy Floyd Hasselbaink

This might seem an odd one from the outset but all I seem to remember as a boy and teenager is the flying Dutchman scoring against us. From his days at Leeds United to his twilight years at Charlton, Hasselbaink always popped up and provided us with untold grief.

But it was his days at Chelsea that aggravated me. Not only did he once score a hat-trick against us at Stamford Bridge, and celebrate like he'd won the World Cup, but in an early season encounter at the Lane he cheated his way to a penalty in a tight 3-2 loss for us.

Chasing a through ball into the box, Hasselbaink caught his foot in the turf as he went to take a shot and tumbled to the ground. The referee, clearly in need of a trip to Specsavers, saw the striker appealing for some reason and blew his whistle pointing to the spot. The nearest defender, Ledley King, looked perplexed, as did the entire crowd as our future captain was a good two or three yards away from the diver when he took a tumble. Then the shameless sod got up and buried his cheated penalty kick. It almost made me beg for VAR back then, that's how much I hate Jimmy Floyd Hasselbaink.

Charlie Adam

Dave Mackay, if he had a neurological accident and acted like a bolting horse on speed.

The Scottish midfielder seemed to be on a one-man mission to injure any Tottenham player that came into his vicinity. In 2011, while we were playing for the right to qualify for Champions League football for the second consecutive season, Adam suddenly saw Gareth Bale as the kind of person who might just sleep with his wife and so proceeded to try and sever his ankle ligaments. Then the following season, having inexplicably earned a move from Blackpool to Liverpool, Adam tried his luck again, slicing through Luka Modrić and Scott Parker in the first half, earning two yellow cards and an early bath.

So, you'd be forgiven in thinking that maybe, after three high-profile incidents involving the same club, he'd keep his head down when the two sides met again on a pre-season tour, but no. Adam tried to kill Gareth Bale again, in a tackle that our Welsh legend later stated he'd never forgive after targetting his ankle for a second time.

By 2013, having moved to Stoke City, he fouled Jan Vertonghen twice and was sent off again. Then in May 2015, he opened the scoring against us in a miserable 3-0 capitulation at the Britannia Stadium. He was resoundingly booed whenever he visited White Hart Lane and rightly so. Adam was a brutal figure and for some reason, seemed to have it in for us. Barely an appearance against us went without incident.

It's amazing to think he never played for any of our London rivals.

Matty Cash

Here's another player who seems to have it in for us, but unlike Charlie Adam, Aston Villa's Poland International, Cash's rash tackles have resulted in career-endangering injuries. In fact, after the right-back's high, dangerous and reckless foul on Rodrigo Bentancur, who was making his first start in nine months after an ACL injury. Our Uruguayan midfielder was then left to face more time on the sidelines and Cash only received a yellow card.

Two seasons earlier, during a 4-0 win for us up at Villa Park, Cash decided that Matt Doherty was far better off in hospital than having a purple patch for our boys when he clattered into his knees with both feet off the ground. Doherty ruptured his MCL and missed the rest of the season. The tackle didn't even warrant a card, or another look with VAR, starting off Cash's reputation on social media and our hatred towards him.

Our feelings are so full of hatred towards him that whenever an encounter with Aston Villa is coming up social media finds new, inventive ways to wish bad things upon him. I just want to see a red card for him at some point. And time in a very dark room with Diamond Lights and children crying being played relentlessly.

John Terry

If you cut John Terry down the middle, he's got Chelsea running through him. That and a deep seething hatred for us.

He loved to wind up our fans. Upon announcing retirement and playing his last game at the Bridge against us, he delighted in posting, "Not on my watch" on Instagram, taking the piss out of our painfully bad record in West London.

He's also been sent off twice against us, both in 2-1 wins and is a general all-round, shameless a-hole. We all know his antics outside of the game and his glory-hunting moments during it after games he had no involvement in. Was there a sweeter sight Terry climbing the Wembley steps as a loser with such sadness across his face when we beat the Chels in the Carling Cup final in 2008 than? He looked like a child who had just witnessed a family of bunny rabbits murdered by a clown.

It was almost a sweeter moment than us lifting the trophy that day.

Daniel Levy

A contentious choice to leave at the end of this chapter. For all the good that Daniel Levy has done, he's also committed to some downright sinful decisions too. I'll explain in this list. I for one will play devil's advocate; he's been good for lots of things and he's been bad for lots of things too. So, as I'm remaining neutral on this, I'll let you decide if he should be on this list or the hero one.

Good

Built the Tottenham Hotspur Stadium.
Built the club globally as a brand.
Under his and ENIC's ownership, we've become challengers in the league, cups and Europe.
Built the worth of the club up from £22 million to £2.8 billion.
Built a state-of-the-art training ground in Enfield.
Helped regenerate the Tottenham area.

Bad

Wanted to move the club to the Olympic Stadium in Stratford to save money on building a new stadium.
Refused to buy players that managers wanted to sign and opted for cheaper alternatives that ultimately failed. This list includes the likes of Jack Grealish, Sergio Aguero, Luis Suarez, Eden Hazard, Samuel E'to, Fernando Morientes, Joao Moutinho, and Paulo Dybala to name but a few.
Didn't buy a single player for 18 months leading up to Tottenham's Champion League final, meaning the club fell back instead of pushed forward.
A pendulum swing between managers who will develop players and when that doesn't work goes for the win now option with no clear focus on the pitch.

Gets too involved in the football side when he's a businessman and always operates best when he leaves that part to someone else.

Has been our chairman during our leanest period for trophies in decades. (One win, four final losses, eight semi-final defeats).

Got us involved in the European Super League.

Appointed Jacques Santini, Josè Mourinho and Antonio Conte.

Told fans he wanted a coach who would bring back our traditional attacking stylish football then appointed Nuno Espirito Santo.

His moments of trying to look like a fan (the cringe ice bucket challenge, COYS Daniel)

Fired Martin Jol with the fans knowing before he did; having confirmed his sacking by text!

Sacked Mauricio Pochettino, our best manager in donkey's years instead of backing him to rebuild.

Sacked Josè Mourinho just days before a cup final.

Furloughed the club's staff during the COVID-19 lockdown to claim back 10% of their wages from the government

Awarded himself a bonus of £3m in 2024, the most of any chairman in the Premier League.

Scrapped the seniors discount on matchday and season tickets and upped ticket prices by, well would you believe it, 6%, which levels out as £3m, which just so happens to be his bonus amount too. Funny, that.

Now if you'll excuse me, I'm going to go and scream into a pillow.

EXTRA TIME

BOOKS AND PODCASTS

Books and podcasts on the club (and the Premier League era in general) that I wholeheartedly recommend:

Books

An Echo of Glory: Tottenham Hotspur in the 21st Century, Gareth Thomas, 2023, Pitch Publishing Ltd, ISBN 978-1801505055

A season-by-season guide which was part of the inspiration for the book that you are reading now. Thanks for reminding me how bad we've had it, Gareth!

Is Gascoigne Going to Have a Crack?: Spurs in the 90s, Magic, Mayhem and Mediocrity, Gareth Dace, 2024, Pitch Publishing Ltd, ISN 978-1801507028

The most comprehensive book on a decade of ups and downs for our beloved club told with the voices of those who were there and, sadly for most, remember it.

Got; Not Got: Spurs: The Lost World of Tottenham Hotspur, Derek Hammond and Gary Silke, 2015, Pitch Publishing Ltd, ISBN 978-1785310744

The collector's almanac. A deep delve into the toys, games, cards, books, figurines and more that have been available for us Spurs fans to consume with all our fandom.

One Step from Glory: Tottenham Hotspur's Champions League Campaign 2018/19, Martin Cloake and Alex Flynn, 2019, Pitch Publishing Ltd, ISBN 978-1785315985

Cloake and Flynn's soaring account of our amazing and yet doomed European run in a very special season. Warning: gets very sad at the end.

Glory, Glory Nights, Adam Powley and Martin Cloake, 2012, Vision Sport Publishing, ISBN 978-1907637667

An update (by 2013 standards) of all our European nights up until 2012-13. Includes interviews with players such as Gareth Bale and Michael Dawson. A brilliant coffee table read of us on the continent.

The Biography of Tottenham Hotspur, Julie Welch, 2016, Vision Sport Publishing, ISBN 978-1909534889

It wouldn't be a Spurs book recommendation list without including one of Welch's works. This has been updated a few times since publication and is a fascinating retelling of our highs and lows heading from birth into the peak of the Poch years.

The Spurs Shirt: The Official History of the Tottenham Hotspur Jersey, Simon Shakeshaft, 2019, Vision Sport Publishing, ISBN 978-1909534766

A fantastic look at the kits and strips we've worn down the years. Includes rare shirts and information hitherto unknown in really astonishing detail.

Spurs Greatest Games: Tottenham Hotspur's Fifty Finest Matches, Mike Donovan, 2012, Pitch Publishing Ltd, ISBN 978-1908051776

Could do with an update now but back in the early 2010s this was a reminder of just how, on our day, we really could beat anybody.

Brave New World: Inside Pochettino's Spurs, Guillem Balague, 2017, Weidenfeld & Nicolson, ISBN 978-1409157717

Warning: Contains lemons.

Tottenham, From the Lane: The Story of Spurs in N17, Kat Lucas, 2021, Pitch Publishing Ltd, ISBN 978-1785318733

Luca's loving historical look at our residency in North London is a great historical retelling of our time on our patch and a little nod to the future.

King: My Autobiography, Ledley King and Mat Snow, 2014, Quercus, ISBN 978-1782069072

Retellings of some of our most formative moments in the Premier League, recounted by the King himself.

Podcasts

These can all be found on your podcasting provider of choice.

The Fighting Cock – Flav, Ricki, T, Big Jon Bass, Alex from Bristol, Spooky et al take an often lewd, crude, light-hearted look at Spurs, with questions from fans that you wouldn't want your Mum to hear.

The Spurs Show – The oldest, arguably most established Tottenham podcast out there as Mike Leigh and Theo Delaney are joined by big-name guests for a topical look at our latest round of fixtures.

The Extra Inch – Imagine if The Fighting Cock got its master's degree and wore elbow patches on their jackets. Windy, his sidekick and best friend Bardi and Nathan A Clark take a tactical deep dive look at our latest and upcoming games.

The Tottenham Way – Sports presenter Marcus Buckland is joined by fellow sports journalists for a weekly look at the goings on at the Tottenham Hotspur Stadium.

When We Were Crap (We Were There) - Only ran for two episodes (come back!) but a game-by-game look at when Spurs were anything less than glory, glory.

Hometown Glory – Ash Sykes, Billie T, Rosa and Sam talk about the latest news and reaction to games, with a focus on the women's team as well as the mens and culture.

The Hotspurs Podcast – Long-running podcast featuring Steve, Colin and Si where they talk with no filter on recent Spurs news, and game reaction with interviews featuring former players and celebrity fans.

The View From The Lane – The Athletic's Jack Pitt-Brooke, Charlie Eccleshare and James Maw bring you guests, news, and insight into the weekly world of Tottenham Hotspur.

Gold and Guest Talk Tottenham – Football.london journalists Alistair Gold and Ro Guest discuss the latest news and journalistic rumblings coming out of N17.

Rule the Roost – Jack (formerly teh_trunk) chats Tottenham with an assortment of guests and also livestreams his hot take reactions of results to his YouTube channel. Hilarious and often cynical in equal measure.

ACKNOWLEDGEMENTS

Firstly, I'd like to thank my wife, Sophie, for putting up with me and my football-mad persona and for always reminding me, when it gets bumpy, that there are more important things in life. This brings me on nicely to my two children, William and Isabelle, who have made supporting Spurs much easier since they have come along. I look forward to ruining your futures by brainwashing you to be lilywhites too! To my Mum, Alison, sisters Clara and Rohanna, brother-in-law, Jordan, nephews Freddie and Loui, father-in-law Gary, Nan and Uncle Roy.

To Anthony Moorin, who for years now has provided such fantastic artwork to my books. A thousand apologies for the extra work you had to do when I forgot to ask for the goalkeeper jerseys to be illustrated! And VC Covers who once again delivered an incredible layout for Anthony's cover art.

To Nick Gill and his family for inviting me along to join them at some of the Wembley games and for the kind permission of the photo of us at the Chelsea FA Cup semi-final. Stephen Rudd and Rob Montgomery for sorting me out with some of the End of Season VHS and DVDs that I was missing from my collection. Watching them back for this book was both a privilege and a chore, depending on which season I was covering! To Jamie Ripper for feedback.

To Chapman and Son in Haverhill for converting the old tapes to DVD to watch for this book.

Prominent Spurs friends over the years Dan Ripley, Chris Pollington, Joey Kettle, Becca Newton, Johnny Martin, Ed Nash and Matt Stewart, Tom Ranson.

I'd also like to thank the podcasts I have listed in the previous chapter and all of the people who have been involved in them. As I grew older, and my Spurs core friendships moved away, they became integral to my fandom and in an odd, sad way, have almost become friends themselves despite us never meeting. Looking forward to bumping into you all some time and having a pint! To Grandad Gribble, for all those times which I wish we still had, I miss them greatly. To Colin Gribble, who hates Chelsea more than any Spurs fan that I know.

A massive thanks should go out to Tottenham Hotspur Football Club, who without them, this book would never have been written...or it'd be about Leyton Orient or Haverhill Rovers or someone like that.

Lastly, and most importantly, to my father Alan. Though you are not here whenever I think of Spurs, which is a lot, I think of you. The times we had and the times that never were. If there is a heaven, I hope your doing a deal with God that sees us winning something really big, really soon! We could all do with the boost, Dad.

Glory, Glory, Hallelujah...and the Spurs Go Marching On...

ABOUT THE AUTHOR

Hayden Gribble was born in Cambridge in the summer of 1989. He spent his formative years obsessed with science fiction, music and football and wrote from an early age. After qualifying as a sports journalist he covered all manner of teams and tournaments, from Premier League, FA Cup, Champions League and World Cup games as a Live Text Commentator for Goal and Eurosport. It was his privilege to cover Tottenham a lot during 2012-2016, and get paid to watch the side he supported since he was five.

In 2012 he wrote his first book, The Man In The Corner, a crime thriller set in the 1960s. Since then he has written 16 books including this one, three of which became Amazon best sellers. He lives in Suffolk with his wife, two children and a wardrobe of Spurs shirts which is starting to creak. He relaxes by walking, spending time with friends and family, playing FIFA and Football Manager, watching cricket and playing guitar. He unrelaxes by watching his beloved Tottenham Hotspur.

His favourite all-time player is Gareth Bale, his all-time favourite manager is Martin Jol and he is known to sing McNamara's Band a lot. His favourite classic albums are Radiohead's OK Computer, De La Soul's 3 Feet High and Rising, The Teardrop Explodes' Kilamanjaro and Blur's Modern Life Is Rubbish. His favourite current acts are Tame Impala, The Weeknd, HAIM, Childish Gambino and Josh Pyke. Kate Bush is his favourite all-time solo artist. Currently he can't seem to stop playing songs by the Small Faces and he holds a life long ambition of being the proud owner of a 1965 Lambretta scooter in white and navy blue and driving his lovely wife Sophie around the country on it.

He dislikes the team from South London, Talksport and anyone who wears half and half scarves that isn't a tourist. His website, where you can find his books, podcasts, radio shows and other work, is
www.haydengribbleauthor.com

His Twitter/X handle is @hayden_gribble and you are welcome to follow him.

Generation to generation…

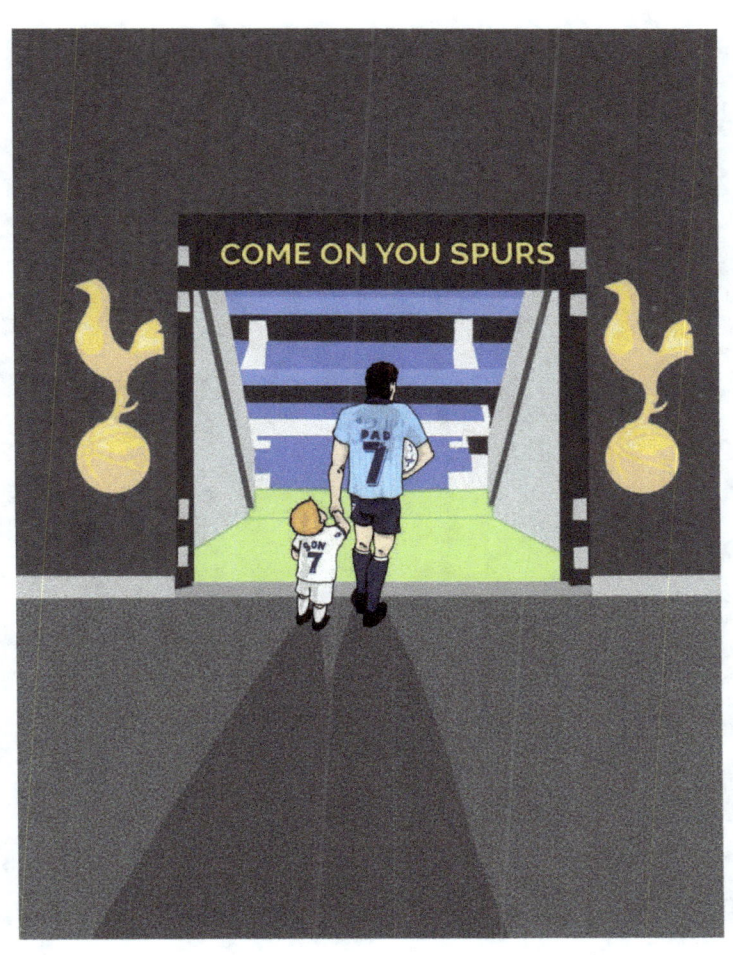

...we go marching on...

www.ingramcontent.com/pod-product-compliance
Lightning Source LLC
Chambersburg PA
CBHW072147070526
44585CB00015B/1030